BINDI IRWIN IS DOWN RIGHT AMAZING

BINDI IRWIN IS DOWN RIGHT AMAZING

AN INTIMATE BIOGRAPHY

JANE FLOWERS

Contents

Introduction

From a young age, Bindi Irwin has captivated the world with her unwavering passion for wildlife and conservation. As the daughter of the late Steve Irwin, one of the most beloved wildlife conservationists and television personalities, Bindi has not only followed in her father's footsteps but has become a role model in her own right.

Bindi not only inherited her father's love for wildlife, but also his unwavering passion for conservation. With her infectious enthusiasm and dedication to protecting our planet's precious creatures, Bindi has become a role model and an influential figure in the world of conservation.

Despite facing unique challenges as someone born with Down syndrome, Bindi's indomitable spirit and dedication to protecting our planet have made her an inspiration to people all over the world.

In this biography we will explore the extraordinary life of

Bindi Irwin and how she continues to make a difference through her work at Australia Zoo and beyond while she continues to ignite a flame of environmental stewardship in young hearts.

Bindi's infectious enthusiasm, coupled with her love for animals, has sparked a flame of environmental stewardship in the hearts of countless children and adults. Her unwavering dedication serves as a reminder that we all have the power to make a difference – no matter our age or circumstances.

While growing up Bindi has been surrounded by animals and immersed in nature at the Australia Zoo in Beerwah Queensland, Australia and it was inevitable that she would develop a deep love for wildlife from an early age. With her father, Steve Irwin who instilled in her a passion for conservation and education before his untimely passing in 2006.

Carrying on her family's legacy, Bindi embraced her role as a wildlife warrior with boundless energy and enthusiasm. From an early age, she became actively involved in various initiatives aimed at raising awareness about endangered species and their habitats. Her infectious personality shone through as she fearlessly handled snakes, cuddled koalas, and interacted with crocodiles – all while wearing the iconic khaki uniforms synonymous with the Irwin family.

From her early days at Australia Zoo to her global activism, Bindi reminds us all of the importance of embracing our passions, advocating for what we believe in, and working together to create a brighter future for our planet.

As Bindi grew older, her undeniable talent for connecting with audiences became evident. She embarked on a successful television career that further amplified her message of conservation.

At just nine years old, she starred in her own wildlife documentary series, "Bindi: The Jungle Girl," where she showcased her knowledge and love for animals to a global audience. Her infectious energy and genuine passion endeared her to viewers of all ages, inspiring them to develop a deeper appreciation for the natural world.

Following the success of her television show, Bindi continued to expand her reach. She appeared on numerous talk shows, spreading awareness about wildlife conservation and emphasizing the importance of protecting our planet's biodiversity. Bindi also took part in various philanthropic endeavors, using her platform to raise funds for conservation projects and promote sustainable practices.

Throughout her journey, Bindi Irwin has become an influential role model for young people around the world. Her ability to navigate life with Down syndrome while pursuing her dreams is a testament to her resilience and determination. Bindi has shown that having a disability does not limit one's potential or ability to make a positive impact on the world.

Through her work as a conservationist, author, and television personality, Bindi has inspired countless children to embrace their passions and actively participate in conservation efforts. She encourages kids everywhere to explore nature, learn about different species, and take action in their own communities.

One of Bindi's most significant contributions lies in her work at Australia Zoo – a wildlife sanctuary founded by her grandparents that serves as both a tourist attraction and a center for research and conservation. As an ambassador for the zoo, Bindi plays an active role in educating visitors about wildlife preservation, highlighting the importance of habitat protection and responsible animal interactions.

At Australia Zoo, Bindi is involved in various initiatives aimed at conserving endangered species. She actively participates in breeding programs focused on threatened animals such as Sumatran tigers and Tasmanian devils. By raising awareness about these vulnerable creatures' plight through educational programs and public appearances, Bindi continues to make a profound impact on wildlife conservation.

Bindi's incredible story serves as a beacon of hope and

inspiration for kids and adults everywhere. It shows them that they too can overcome adversity, embrace their passions, and make a positive impact on the world around them. Bindi's journey is a testament to the power of perseverance, compassion, and the belief that one person can truly make a difference.

Let Bindi Irwin's story be a reminder to us all of the importance of embracing our passions, advocating for what we believe in, and working together to create a brighter future for our planet. In a world that often feels overwhelming, Bindi's unwavering dedication and love for wildlife serve as a guiding light, reminding us of the beauty that can be found when we care for and protect the natural world.

1

CHAPTER 1

———

Now let's take a closer look at the inspiring life of Bindi Irwin, a true wildlife warrior who follows in the footsteps of her parents, Terri and Steve Irwin.

Wildlife Warrior and Conservationist Bindi Sue Irwin was born on July 24, 1998 in Buderim, Queensland, Australia to (Steve) Stephen Robert Irwin, affectionately known as "The Crocodile Hunter". Steve is from Essendon, Australia and Bindi's mom is Terri Reiner Irwin from Eugene, Oregon in the USA. Bindi was also born with Down Syndrome, yet she and her family have never publicly acknowledged about the fact that Bindi was born with Down Syndrome. It is unclear as to what kind of Down Syndrome Bindi was born with, but I suspect she was born with Mosaic Down Syndrome.

Bindi was named after her dad's favorite crocodile kept at the Australia Zoo. Bindi is also an aboriginal term meaning "little girl". Her middle name Sue came from her dad's dog Sui, who died from Cancer on June 23, 2004 at the ripe old age of 15 years old. She has English, Irish, and Swedish ancestors, with a heavy Irish influence on her father's side.

While growing up in Australia Zoo, Bindi developed a special bond with the animals that surrounded her, learning from her father how to care for them. Through her parents' teachings, she quickly gained an understanding of nature's intricate balance and began to realize the importance of conservation.

Before Bindi was born her mother, Terri, was 27 years old and her father, Steve, was 29 years old when they married a year after they met in 1991. They first met when Terri was a tourist in Australia visiting the Beerwah, Queensland area. At the time Steve was performing a crocodile demonstration at the Australia Zoo.

It was a spur of the moment decision for Terri to stop at the Zoo while on her trip touring Australia where she first met Steve. Terri would later comment on an episode of Crocodile Hunter, *"There was a crocodile demonstration going on with this* guy", "*This man was with a crocodile talking about animals the way you talk about what you had for lunch.*"

As the demonstration was performing Steve commented out loud,"*And now I'm going to feed this crocodile. Isn't he a little beauty?.*" While he was commenting Terri said that she thought, "*Well, I never really thought of crocodiles as beautiful, but I'll have a look.*"

Then Terri noticed Steve handed the crocodile some food and that the crocodile came quickly screaming out of the water towards Steve before grabbing the piece of food. Terri commented that she noticed Steve was as calm as if he was mailing a letter in a letter box. That's when she knew she was sold, with Terri commenting ,"*I thought this man is the most incredible guy I have ever seen*", "*He's probably married*", He's got to be taken.*"

It was love at first sight for Terri and Steve. Steve was equally as smitten from the moment he set eyes on his future wife. With Steve commenting about the first time when he met Terri claiming "*When I saw Terri in the crowd*", "*I looked up and our eyes met and my heart just went, 'BANG, BANG, BANG, BANG,' just starting thumping*", "*It was love at first sight*".

Steve went on to comment, "*I know this sounds like it's coming out of some Mills and Boone love novel, but it's true....So I wound up the demo – 'Yep, thanks for coming – and then she stayed back and talked to me."*

Steve Irwin and Terri Irwin when they first met (Photo credit: Steve Irwin)

Terri has commented in the past after she first met Steve that he asked her an important question when he revealed he was single in a pretty cheeky way.

Terri said, *"When Steve and I met, he asked me"*, *"would you like to meet my girlfriend?"*

Terri commented at the time, *"I just felt utterly crushed, and then he called out, 'hey, Suey,' and here comes this little dog, Suey." ,"I went, 'Boom! No girlfriend!'"*

After dating for a year Steve and Terri were later engaged on February 3, 1992 and would eventually marry in Terri's hometown of Eugene, Oregon in June of 1992.

For their honeymoon, since the couple were so equally interested in animal conservation. They spent it on a crocodile rescue mission filming documentaries, with a film crew in tow, which is how their documentary series The Crocodile Hunter began.

The Australia Zoo has always been Bindi's home. Bindi made her first television debut on The Crocodile Hunter and by 2002 at the age of four years old with Bindi appearing regularly in her father's television show, "The Crocodile Hunter Diaries."

While Bindi was growing up at the Australia Zoo her dad recorded many short takes of his daughter in Australia. What better way to tell the story of how Bindi was growing up at the Australia Zoo than through the short takes filmed by her dad, Steve Irwin .

With Bindi commenting in the past, *"Since I can remember, my life has been captured on camera"* ,*"I was literally filmed being born"*, *"That was exciting,"*

You see the intimate moments of Bindi's growth on film shared by the Australia Zoo. There were posted takes of Bindi growing up seen on YouTube in a video posted by the Irwins called Baby Bindi Irwin| Irwin Family Adventures. The video shared precious behind-the-scenes moments captured on

Terri's handycam while they were discovering the marvelous world of wildlife.

With Bindi's dad speaking to Bindi during the filming of these intimate moments of Bindi, commenting about how she wanted to be just like her dad, that were caught by her dad and mom on film. The takes caught how she was growing up learning to be just like her dad, The Crocodile Hunter.

During the filming Steve said, *"Baby Bindi is the light of our life and like every proud parent"*, *"We've revealed all the growing up milestones"*, *"Just like every kid she is fascinated by animals and not only the one's one finds at the zoo and me I am the proudest dad in the world. No doubt about it"*, *"She's growing up"*, *"Unafraid of what other kids would normally find creepy or frightening"*, *"You'd expect a love of animals, but Bindi also loves the little girly things all girls love and just uncle (Stan wears) what is this?"*, *"At the zoo. She loves dressing up and being the family star"*, *"Hey Bindi. Who do you want to be when you grow up?"*

Bindi replied, *"I want to be like my daddy."*

Steve was so happy to hear this and he exclaimed, *"Yeah, and she already is Crikey"*, *"She just grew up turning into dad"*, *Loves all animals"*, *"Don't you babe?"*

Bindi replied with, *"Yeah."*

Steve remarked, *"From cougars, to snakes and crocodiles"*, *"How about Bugs?"*

Bindi shyly replied, "Yes."

Steve also asked, *"Spiders?"*

"Yes", replied Bindi.

"I remember this time we're out in the desert and you cried because I wanted you to put the spider back in the bush where it lived", *"Do you remember that?"*, asked Steve.

"Yes", replied Bindi.

Steve chuckled in excitement, *"He, he, he . All creatures great and small"*, *"That's my girl."*

As time went by Bindi also had an appearance in the film "The Wiggles: Wiggly Safari" in a video called Bindi Irwin: Self. It was the Wiggles 12th video special. In collaboration with the Fab four.

The Wiggles were joined by their friends Steve Irwin, Terri

and Bindi Irwin on a wonderful adventurous safari at the Australia Zoo. The special was released on July 8, 2002.

If you were a child in the early 2000s, chances are you've heard of The Wiggles. This Australian children's music group captured the hearts of kids worldwide with their catchy tunes and vibrant personalities. But did you know that they once embarked on a wild adventure called "Wiggly Safari" alongside the iconic Irwin family?

The Wiggles 12th video special was filmed in collaboration with the Irwin Family at the Australia Zoo and was released on July 8, 2002. It was produced by Paul Field and Gary Mathisen and the Executive Producers were The Wiggles.

In "Wiggly Safari," The Wiggles were joined by their usual lineup – Murray Wiggle (Murray Cook), Jeff Wiggle (Jeff Fatt), Anthony Wiggle (Anthony Field), and Greg Wiggle (Greg Page).

This extraordinary production brought together the beloved children's entertainers with their friends Steve Irwin, Terri Irwin, and their daughter Bindi Irwin. Together with The Wiggles, they embarked on an unforgettable journey through the Australia Zoo.

Filmed at the Australia Zoo, known for its dedication to wildlife conservation and education, this video showcased an exciting safari filled with laughter, learning, and lots of wiggling.

You also see dancing with Dorothy the Dinosaur: Corrine O'Rafferty and the Butterflies and dancing the Dingo Tango with Wags the Dog: Andrew McCourt and singing with Henry the Octopus: Reem Hanwell.. All of the friends of The Wiggles became part of The Crocodile band.

The songs featured in the album are The Crocodile Hunter, Australia Zoo, Wobbly Camel, Cocky, Want A Cracker, Butterflies Flit, Dorothy Queen of the Roses (In Concert), Swim With Me, Koala La La, Dingo Tango, You Might Like A Pet, Old Man Emu (John Williamson cover), Feeding Time, Do The Owl, Kookaburra Choir, Snakes (You Can Look, But You Better Not Touch) We're The Crocodile Band.

Wiggle Safari is the 14th album released from an Australian children's music group. The album was also nominated for Best Children's Album ARIA in 2002 but unfortunately lost to Hi – 5 Boom Beat.

As expected from The Wiggles, "Wiggle Safari" was packed with catchy songs that celebrated Australia's unique wildlife. From crocodiles to koalas, each song introduced children to different animals and their habitats. Some of the memorable tunes featured in the album include "The Crocodile Hunter," "Koala La La," and "Dingo Tango." The Wiggles' friends also joined in on the fun, with Dorothy the Dinosaur dancing, Wags the Dog tangoing, and Henry the Octopus lending his melodious voice.

Beyond the music and cheerful dance numbers, "Wiggly Safari" aimed to educate young viewers about wildlife conservation and appreciation. With Steve Irwin's expertise and passion for animals shining through, children were not only entertained but also inspired to care for our planet's incredible biodiversity. The collaboration between The Wiggles and the Irwin family brought attention to the importance of preserving Australia's unique fauna.

"Wiggly Safari" marked another success in The Wiggles' extensive discography. Although it did not win Best Children's Album at ARIA in 2002, its nomination showcased its impact on young audiences across Australia. This collaboration between two beloved Australian families left a lasting impression on fans around the world, solidifying Bindi Irwin's place as a rising star.

As we reflect on this magical adventure that brought together The Wiggles and Bindi Irwin, let us remember the joy it brought to countless children. Through catchy songs, infectious enthusiasm, and important messages about wildlife conservation, "Wiggly Safari" continues to inspire younger generations to appreciate nature's wonders.

Also in 2002 Steve and Bindi had an appearance on the Winfrey Show that showcased an Unforgettable Wildlife Conservation Moment, with the show televised across the nation that was captivated by the fearless Australian wildlife expert, Steve Irwin, known by many as 'The Crocodile Hunter.'

In a truly unforgettable episode of 'The Oprah Winfrey Show,' Steve Irwin, accompanied by his then 4-year-old daughter, Bindi Irwin, took center stage. The dynamic duo not only showcased their undeniable charm but also used this platform to shed light on the importance of wildlife conservation. Today, we take a nostalgic journey back to that remarkable episode and explore the lasting impact it had on both viewers and the conservation movement.

During the captivating episode on 'The Oprah Winfrey Show,' audiences were treated to a unique sight with Steve sharing his passion with his young daughter Bindi by his side. Together, they mesmerized viewers with their engaging personalities and genuine love for wildlife. This appearance showcased not only their familial bond but also the passing of the torch to a new generation of conservationists.

With his larger-than-life personality and unwavering

passion for wildlife, Steve managed to capture hearts worldwide. He brought viewers close to nature's most awe-inspiring creatures, all while educating them about their significance in our ecosystem.

At just four years old, Bindi Irwin stole the show on "The Oprah Winfrey Show" with her infectious enthusiasm and adorable presence. The world watched as she fearlessly interacted with various animals, showcasing her father's teachings and passion for wildlife. This was only the beginning of a remarkable journey for Bindi, who would go on to become an influential figure in her own right.

Bindi's appearance on 'The Oprah Winfrey Show' introduced her to a global audience, paving the way for her future endeavors in wildlife conservation and education. Today, she carries on her father's legacy through numerous initiatives, including running Australia Zoo and starring in television series that continue to educate viewers about the importance of protecting our planet's precious creatures.

Beyond the entertainment value of seeing Steve and Bindi Irwin in action, their appearance on 'The Oprah Winfrey Show' served a higher purpose – raising awareness about wildlife conservation. Steve passionately spoke about the urgent need to protect endangered species and their habitats. He emphasized that every individual has a role to play in preserving our planet's biodiversity for future generations.

One of Steve Irwin's greatest strengths was his ability to educate and inspire others to take action. During this special episode, he shared stories of his close encounters with wildlife while emphasizing the importance of respecting and appreciating these magnificent creatures. His sheer dedication and genuine love for animals resonated deeply with viewers, motivating many to become more actively involved in conservation efforts themselves.

Steve believed that by fostering an understanding and appreciation for nature at an early age, we could instill lifelong values of compassion and environmental stewardship. Through his work alongside Bindi during their appearance on 'The Oprah Winfrey Show,' this message reached millions, further fueling the conservation movement.

The episode featuring Steve and Bindi Irwin on 'The Oprah Winfrey Show' was undoubtedly a watershed moment for wildlife conservation. It brought the urgent need for action to the forefront of public consciousness and inspired countless individuals to become advocates for our planet's precious ecosystems.

As we reflect on that remarkable appearance of Steve and Bindi on 'The Oprah Winfrey Show,' may it serve as a call to action for each of us. Their Appearance left us with a lasting memory that we should all become stewards of our environment, protecting the incredible biodiversity that exists all around us. Then together, we can ensure that future generations will also have the opportunity to marvel at the wonders of nature just as we did when the Irwins grace our screens that unforgettable day in 2002.

When it comes to the Irwin family, their passion for wildlife conservation and their deep love for each other have always been at the forefront of their lives and as time went by Terri would later become pregnant with her and Steve's second child. She had the sweetest way when she told Steve the joyful news she was pregnant with their second child. The footage of her telling Steve was captured on film and released by Animal Planet.

You see in footage of Terri's pregnancy journey, with Baby Bob, her commenting to Steve while she was eating in 2003, *"I don't know why, I just have these cravings."* Terri commented to Steve as she chewed on pickles and ice cream.

Steve caught on right away and exclaimed, *"Woohoo!"*, *"I've bloody done it!"*, before hugging his friend (Mate) Wes after commenting, *"I'll congratulate my mate first."*

Then Steve leaned forward and kissed and hugged his wife

while he expressed his surprise that they were having another baby. Immediately afterwards Steve called his Grammy and shouted loudly over the phone call ,"*Guess What*", "*You wouldn't believe what just happened*", "*Do you remember that information you gave Terri about getting pregnant?*", "*It worked*", "*I am serious*", "*She is eating ice cream right.*"

Then after he got off the phone with his Grammy he called his dad exclaiming to his dad," *Hey, Dad. I've got news*", "*This morning she (Terri) is eating ice cream*", "*Do you know what I mean?*"

Then if that wasn't enough for Steve. He then told the whole world his wife Terri was pregnant when he commented to a crowd at the Australia Zoo while the audience was watching him feed his crocodile Graham. Steve exclaimed, "*How's this?*", "*How's this speaking of which Terri is pregnant.*"

The news of Terri's pregnancy came as a delightful surprise to both her and Steve. After years of dedicating themselves to their conservation efforts and raising their beloved daughter Bindi, they were overjoyed at the prospect of expanding their family. Little did they know that this precious moment would be forever cherished by millions around the world.

It was an ordinary day in the Irwin household when Terri mustered up the courage to share her exciting secret with Steve. Unbeknownst to him, she had arranged for a special surprise that would capture his genuine reaction. As the cameras rolled and anticipation filled the air, Terri broke the news that she was expecting another child – Baby Bob was on the way!

Terri's pregnancy journey was filled with many emotions – excitement, anticipation, and even moments of reflection. As she prepared to welcome Baby Bob into the world, she embraced each milestone with grace and gratitude.

Throughout her pregnancy with Baby Bob, Terri prioritized both her physical and emotional well-being. From maintaining a balanced diet to engaging in gentle exercise routines suitable for expectant mothers, she ensured that Baby Bob received the utmost care right from the start.

With every kick, hiccup, and ultrasound appointment held a special place in Terri's heart as she cherished these precious moments of connection with her unborn child. Her excitement grew as she envisioned how this new addition would further strengthen their family bond and continue Steve's incredible legacy.

As news of Terri's pregnancy spread far and wide, an outpouring of love and support flooded in from fans around the globe. The Irwin family had become an inspiration to many, showcasing a harmonious blend of dedication to wildlife conservation and unwavering love for one another.

With each passing day, the world grew more eager to meet Baby Bob – a symbol of hope, resilience, and boundless love. As Terri continued her journey toward motherhood, we stood alongside the Irwin family, celebrating this new chapter and eagerly awaiting the arrival of their precious bundle of joy, Baby Bob.

Terri would later give birth to Bindi's little brother "Baby Bob" Robert Clarence Irwin on December 1st, 2003 in Buderim, Australia. Robert was named after Terri's dad and Steve's dad. The birth of Robert was one of the most important highlights of Steve and Terri's life and was the biggest milestone for everyone at the Australia Zoo and especially Terri's family.

After Robert was born Steve went to pick up Bindi to take her to see her little brother and give her the good news. Once Bindi arrived at the hospital to see and hold her new little brother she started taking everything in stride li+ke a big sister should do as she adjusted to her baby brother.

Bindi wasn't convinced right yet when she saw her little brother that he was actually a boy and she asked her mom while holding her little brother on her lap, *"How do you know he's a boy?"*

Terri responded, *"Because we know."*

Bindi asked, *"Did you check?"*, *"How long is he going to sleep for?"*, *"I think by the way he is, I'll call him Brian."*

Steve looked Bindi straight in the eye and said, *"His name is Robert"*.

Bindi responded, *"But I'll call him Brian for short."*

Steve responded to Bind with, *"Ok"*

Life at that moment in time when Robert was born could never have been more perfect than the magical moment. Steve had so much joy in his life after Robert was born. With the arrival of baby Bob, Steve and terrie's life was complete, and they cherished the new addition to their family.

Shortly after his birth, Steve held Robert in his arms at the hospital while claiming that the whole reason we were put on earth was to hold your newborn baby or so it seems that way.

After the birth of Robert it wasn't too long before the news was going around the Australia Zoo and afterwards there was a photo shoot for Robert, who Steve and Terri called Baby Bob. The photo shoot was held to announce to the world the birth of Baby Bob.

Afterwards Steve showed off Baby Bob to a crowd of people at the Australia Zoo. You could also hear Bindi's adorable voice singing Rockabye Baby in the tree top to her little brother to help console him while he was crying in his dad's hands. Then quickly Steve handed Baby Bob to Terri so she could help to console him while he cried.

Terri would later comment she felt like she was the mother who handed her baby over onto the altar to be sacrificed or so to speak. Many people thought of it like that when Terri thought of it as like a family event that was a joyful one that she and Steve wanted to share with everyone in the Crocoseum at the Australia Zoo.

But Steve received criticism from social media outlets because he took Baby Bob out when he fed his crocodile, Murray in the Crocoseum. Steve had all his family with him when he was feeding Murray with baby Bob and also he had a group of visiting Buddhist nuns there to bless Bob in a fantastic ceremony.

Baby Bob's birth and presentation to the world completed the Irwin family and was the highlight of Steve and Terri's life. Many adventures awaited the Irwin's in the coming years. Adventures with animal conservation.

As Baby Bob grew, many adventures awaited him and his family, particularly in the realm of animal conservation. Steve and Terri, being passionate about wildlife and nature, likely instilled these values in their son from a young age.

Terri, Bindi, Robert and Steve Irwin (Photo credit: The Australia Zoo)

After the birth of Robert, Baby Bob, Bindi continued to be homeschooled in the Australian Outback so she could travel with her father and help him film his popular nature shows like "The Crocodile Hunter."

2

CHAPTER 2

———————

Unfortunately as time went by, while Bindi was growing up in the Australian Outback, her father Steve Irwin lost his life from a Bull Ray piercing through his heart with its lethal barb. Known for his fearless approach to nature and infectious enthusiasm, Steve had touched the lives of millions around the globe. His tragic death was accidental and extraordinarily rare because the last time in Australia when someone was ever struck in the chest by a StingRay barb was in the 1940s. This rarity adds to the gravity and uniqueness of this tragedy. While such incidents are incredibly rare, it is important to understand the unique circumstances surrounding this unfortunate event.

In 2006, the world lost a beloved icon whose passion for

wildlife and infectious enthusiasm captivated millions. Steve Irwin, renowned as "The Crocodile Hunter," met an untimely demise in an accident that shocked the world.

The world was left in shock when Steve's tragic death occurred on September 4th, 2006, while he was setting up to shoot ocean reef footage for one of his shows, fate dealt a devastating blow to Steve Irwin. Accompanied by a crew on his vessel named "Crock One," Steve embarked on what would become his final adventure.

The Croc One (Photo credit: Sunshine Coast Daily with The Courier Mail from the article Ghost ship returns without skippier: Croc One makes a silent journey back into the canals)

His trusted cameraman and partner of over 15 years, Steve's right hand man Justin Lyons, was by his side as they worked on a documentary called "Ocean's Deadliest" which aimed to showcase marine life found in reefs. Their plan was to capture thrilling footage featuring sharks, crocodiles, Blue-Ring Octopus, Box Jellyfish, and even milking sea snakes.

During their break from filming scenes for eight consecutive days that were brimming with danger and excitement, Steve Irwin and Justin Lyons decided to venture out onto the water using a raft from their main vessel. Driven by their insatiable curiosity and thirst for discovery, they embarked on a quest to find Tiger sharks for their next filming endeavor. However, little did they know that this seemingly innocuous decision would lead to an unimaginable tragedy.

As fate would have it, Steve's life took an unexpected turn when he found himself face-to-face with a Bull Ray covered in sand. In an unfortunate twist of events, as Steve approached the creature from above, the Bull Ray's barbed tail rose swiftly, striking him directly in the chest. This harrowing encounter proved fatal, with the barb piercing Steve's heart and robbing the world of an extraordinary individual.

The final memory of Steve Irwin, as recalled by his friend Justin, paints a haunting picture of the renowned wildlife enthusiast in his last moments. With a calm demeanor, Steve uttered the chilling words "I'm dying" before departing this world. This poignant statement serves as a somber reminder of the fragility of life and the suddenness with which it can be taken away. It encapsulates the vulnerability and mortality that even larger-than-life figures like Irwin are not immune to.

In the aftermath of Steve's untimely demise, his tragic death was captured on film by Justin Lyons. However, one of his former friends, John Stanton, voiced strong opposition to ever releasing this footage to the public. Stanton believed that such a distressing portrayal of Steve's final moments should never be aired, deeming it too painful and disturbing for viewers to witness.

There was an interview called Steve Irwin's Last Words: Interview with his Underwater Cameraman Part 1 on Studio 10 with one of Steve's former friends, John Stanton. John stated in the interview that he saw the film of Steve's accidental death recorded by Justin Lyons and he stated he didn't want Steve's horrible death that was filmed to ever be aired because he thought it was just a horrible piece of film to be viewed.

John Stanton said that Steve was coming around over the top of the Bull Ray that was covered in the sand when the Bull Ray's barbed tail came up and went straight into Steve's chest.

John doesn't remember anything after that or so he said in an interview with ABC's Barbara Walters called Tragedy in Australia: The Steve Irwin story. How is it that Justin and John have contradicting stories of what was happening on the day and that week when Steve died?

Justin said that it had been eight rainy days into filming and because it had been rainy when he and Steve decided to take a break because they were bored. Justin stated that Steve felt like a caged tiger when he was on the mother boat the "Crock One" and because Steve felt like a caged tiger, they got in the raft and went to film Tiger sharks.

However, John stated that it was a sunny day when they were out filming and there were two or three days of beautiful sunshine when they were out filming bendy shows on Bat Reef. So as you can see these are contradicting accusations of what was occurring up until the time Steve died.

Steve can be seen in the last known photos of him before his death on his raft with his cameraman John Lyons on Bat Reef. These photos can be seen on social media. In one of the photos Steve is giving the okay sign on his raft before he dives in the water to film Tiger Sharks.

Steve Irwin (Photo credit: Youtube video Steve Irwin Last Video – 1 Day Before Death taken from FreshVirals)

In another photo Steve can be seen directing his raft with his crew before he gives the Okay sign and then he dives into the water to film Tiger Sharks.

Steve Irwin (Photo credit: Youtube video Steve Irwin Last Video – 1 Day Before Death taken from FreshVirals)

In a YouTube video John Stanton stated that he saw Steve pulling out the Barb that stabbed him in his chest, but Justin Lyons said the Bull Ray Barb pierced Steve's chest stabbed

Steve hundreds of times within a few seconds wildly through Steve's chest and Steve did not pull the Barb out!

So John and Justin's claims are contradicting stories of how their Mate Steve Irwin died and how the weather was that day and that week. So how are you going to pull out a barb with your hands like John stated, but Justin stated that the Barb pierced Steve hundreds of times within seconds and then the Ray swam off. So whose claim is the real and the factual claim of how Steve really died?

The accounts detailing the exact sequence of events leading to Steve's death have varied, leaving many puzzled about what truly transpired that day. One account comes from John Stanton, a former friend of Steve's who claimed to have seen Justin Lyons' recorded footage of the incident. Stanton asserted that Steve was swimming above the Bull Ray, which was partially buried in sand when its barbed tail struck him in the chest.

As we attempt to unravel this tragic event in search for clarity , it is important to note conflicting testimonies. While John Stanton's claim suggests a scenario where Steve could potentially remove the barb himself, Justin Lyons provided a different perspective. According to Lyons, the barb pierced Steve multiple times within seconds before the Ray swam away—an account that implies swift and forceful strikes.

The conflicting accounts emerged, leaving many puzzled about the true sequence of events. As we delve deeper into uncovering the circumstances surrounding Steve Irwin's passing, it becomes evident that finding absolute certainty may prove challenging. With conflicting testimonies and disputed details, piecing together an ironclad narrative is no easy task. Yet, what remains unchanged is our collective grief for losing a remarkable individual who dedicated his life to wildlife conservation and education.

With the conflicting narratives surrounding Steve's final moments. They only deepen the mystery surrounding his untimely death. One would think that to uncover the truth behind this tragedy, further investigation and analysis are required, but regardless of how Steve met his unfortunate end, his legacy as a wildlife warrior and passionate advocate for conservation lives on. His infectious enthusiasm and unwavering dedication continue to inspire people worldwide to appreciate and protect our natural world.

In conclusion, while the exact details of how Steve Irwin died from a Bull Ray piercing his heart may forever remain somewhat shrouded in uncertainty, however one thing is clear: his legacy as a passionate advocate for nature and wildlife will continue to inspire generations to come. Let us remember him not only for his tragic end, but also for the countless lives he touched and the profound impact he made during his time with us.

The loss of Steve Irwin was a blow felt by countless individuals who had been touched by his work and infectious personality. As we reflect on his life and untimely passing, it is imperative not only to honor his memory, but also to continue championing the causes he held dear. Let us celebrate his remarkable contributions while striving to preserve our planet for future generations—just as he did throughout his extraordinary life.

Despite the heartbreaking circumstances surrounding Steve's passing, his legacy continues to shine brightly. Through his boundless passion for wildlife conservation and education, he left an indelible mark on both individuals and communities worldwide. Today, we remember Steve not only for his unforgettable television persona but also for his unwavering dedication to protecting our planet's precious ecosystems.

Steve also captured hearts around the world with his infectious enthusiasm for wildlife and his unwavering commitment to conservation. Through his television shows and charismatic personality, he became a beloved figure who educated and entertained millions. His untimely passing in 2006 left a void in both his family's life and in the hearts of people worldwide.

However, rather than succumbing to grief or fading from public view after Steve's untimely passing, Terri Irwin and their children, Bindi and Robert, carried forward Steve's legacy with incredible strength and determination. They continued their work at Australia Zoo while also becoming advocates for wildlife conservation themselves.

As we reflect on this tragic incident that claimed the life of a true legend, let us honor Steve Irwin's memory by carrying forward his mission of safeguarding our natural world. May his spirit inspire us all to appreciate and protect the incredible biodiversity that surrounds us.

At the time when Steve died, his wife Terri was traveling with their kids Bindi and Robert. Once they got to their destination Terri received an urgent message from her brother-in-law. He told her in the message that there had been an accident and that Steve had died.

Terri was in complete disbelief and shock when she heard that Steve died and the only thing that she could remember was herself saying *"Don't Say It!"* over and over again in her head. Afterwards Terri told her daughter Bindi her father had just passed away and to always remember.

Later Terri stated to Barbara Walters that she told Bindi that we can be Wildlife Warriors after the accidental death of Steve.

Terri Irwin (Photo credit: ABC News with Barbara Walters)

When something goes wrong. You have to have faith and have to believe that it can be a new chapter and that we can go on. We can understand grief, but we will not be victims of this grief that we are understanding. That we will be Wildlife Warriors!

As time went by after Steve's death Terri went on to carry on Steve's message that he stood for family and Wildlife. She wanted everyone to celebrate Steve's life and what he stood for because there's so much more to Steve and everyone should know about his legacy and what he left behind.

Terri lost her Prince when Steve died from a Bull Ray piercing his heart. In his honor of her late husband Terri started the Steve Irwin Day that comes around every year on November 15th.

I for one enjoy celebrating this day when it comes around. I am a fan of Steve Irwin, "The Crocodile Hunter" and Terri is right. He did stand for wildlife and I am going to stand along with him and be a Wildlife Warrior too.

There is no video evidence anywhere of Steve dying. If there is any evidence it could possibly be kept private with Terri and her family, but Terri has stated that she destroyed the film of Steve dying after the police viewed it. Some people don't believe that Terri actually destroyed the footage, but I guess we'll never really know for sure and the only person that knows is Terri.

Later that month on September 20 Bindi received a standing ovation after delivering a Eulogy for her dad in front of a crowd of 5,000 and in front of a television audience of more than 300 million viewers.

It was the Irwin family's first public appearance since Steve's death on Sept. 4. Terri sat with Robert and was joined by their family friend Wes Mannion while Bindi took center stage in front of a crowd that greeted her with a standing ovation and cheers of encouragement from 5,000 friends and family sitting in the Crocoseum in the Australia Zoo while Bindi showed no signs of fear or nervousness what so ever before millions of viewers giving her Eulogy speech to honor her father.

8 year old Bindi Irwin delivering her father's Eulogy speech)
(Photo credit: OWN Oprah website)

Bindi said during her speech, "My Daddy was my hero – he was always there for me when I needed him", "He listened to me and taught me so many things, but most of all he was fun", "I know that Daddy had an important job", "He was working to change the world so everyone would love wildlife like he did", "He built a hospital to help animals and he bought lots of land to give animals a safe place to live."

"He took me and my brother and my Mum with him all the time."

"We filmed together, caught crocodiles together and loved being in the bush together", "I don't want Daddy's passion to ever end", "I want to help endangered wildlife just like he did."

"I have the best Daddy in the whole world and I will miss him every day", "When I see a crocodile I will always think of him and I know that Daddy made this zoo so everyone could come and learn to love *all the animals", "Daddy made this place his whole life and now it's our turn to help Daddy."*

Many people were moved by Bindi's speech to her dad. She was very composed and confident while giving her speech. Her ability to write and deliver a Eulogy at her dad's funeral is a very rare skill indeed. Writing a Eulogy can be one of the most difficult speeches to write and Bindi wrote a great speech as a mark of respect for her dad.

After Bindi's speech she received a standing ovation by the people that attended Steve Irwin's tribute at the Australia Zoo's Crocoseum. Steve's Mate John Stanton has claimed Bindi wrote the Eulogy all by herself with no one's help.

Her speech took less than a minute to deliver and was less than one page. Yet her tribute to her dad will always be remembered for having moved the world and was a great memorable speech.

Bindi was herself when she spoke the words in her speech. She helped everyone remember life's achievements and her dad's legacy while she focused on the awards, recognition and what her dad achieved in his lifetime.

She made a memorable statement that everyone will remember including the media. It's her words that we will remember. With her stating, *"My Daddy was my hero – he was always there for me when I needed him."* Bindi's speech touched the hearts of people all over the world when she told her personal story. Her story provided an emotional and a visual link into the life of her and her dad.

Bindi's speech was brief and to the point while she kept a confident and calm composer. She passed a milestone for her to be able to say a speech and tribute to her father in front of a camera and crowd many times over because of the way she was raised and brought up by her dad and Mum.

People of all ages learned from Bindi's wonderful speech. Even though Bindi was 8 years old and had Down Syndrome she was still able to express how she felt clearly about her father's passing in her speech and understandably while she moved the world.

After Steve's untimely death, Bindi started following in his footsteps more than ever before. She appeared on the cover of the Australian magazine New Idea's 104 year history in September 2006. Bindi is the youngest person in the magazine's 104-year history to appear on the cover of the magazine.

It was September 2006 when Bindi, a bright young star, graced the cover of the iconic Australian magazine, New Idea.

At just eight years old, Bindi made history as the youngest person ever to appear on the cover in the publication's impressive 104-year history.

Bindi's appearance on New Idea's cover marked a historic moment not only for her but also for the magazine itself. At just eight years old, she broke records by becoming the youngest person ever featured on its cover. This achievement was a testament to her growing influence as a young environmentalist and conservationist.

The cover story showcased Bindi's infectious smile, her love for animals, and her determination to carry on her father's work. It was a powerful statement that highlighted the immense potential of this young star and foreshadowed the impact she would have in the years to come.

While Bindi undoubtedly carries forward her father's legacy, she has also forged her own path and emerged as an influential figure in her own right. Beyond being recognized as Steve Irwin's daughter, Bindi has established herself as a passionate advocate for conservation, a talented television presenter, and an inspirational role model for young people around the world.

Following in her father's footsteps, Bindi has dedicated herself to wildlife conservation from a young age. Through Australia Zoo, the family-owned sanctuary on the Sunshine Coast of Queensland, she actively participates in animal care and rescue efforts. Bindi's unwavering commitment to preserving biodiversity and protecting endangered species is evident through her involvement with various organizations and initiatives.

Bindi's captivating presence extends beyond magazine covers. She has appeared in numerous television shows over the years, showcasing not only her passion for wildlife but also her infectious energy and charisma. With programs like "Bindi: The Jungle Girl" and "Crikey! It's the Irwins," she has captured audiences worldwide, inspiring viewers with her knowledge, love for animals, and dedication to environmental causes.

Through these platforms, Bindi has become an international ambassador for wildlife conservation. Her ability to connect with people of all ages and backgrounds is a testament to her genuine desire to educate, inspire change, and make a positive impact on our planet.

As an adult audience witnessing Bindi's incredible journey unfold over the years, we cannot help but be inspired by this remarkable young woman. From her groundbreaking appearance on New Idea's cover as a child to her present-day achievements, Bindi embodies the spirit of determination, compassion, and resilience.

Her commitment to carrying on her father's legacy while forging her own path serves as a testament to the power of passion and purpose. Bindi has proven that age is no barrier when it comes to making a difference and inspiring change.

Bindi's appearance on the cover of Australian magazine New Idea was not just a historic moment but also a glimpse into the future of wildlife conservation. Through her unwavering dedication, infectious enthusiasm, and global influence, she has become an influential figure in her own right. As we witness Bindi's ongoing journey, we are reminded of the indelible impact one person can make in shaping a better world for future generations. Let us continue supporting Bindi and celebrating her incredible contributions to wildlife conservation and environmental advocacy.

3

CHAPTER 3

In a heartwarming and courageous moment, Bindi took the stage at the Nickelodeon Australian Kids Choice Awards at the Sydney Entertainment Centre, in Sydney Australia on October 11, 2006. Despite the recent and tragic loss of her beloved father, Steve Irwin, Bindi showed incredible strength as she presented the Favorite Aussie Award to Guy Sebastian.

This event was not just any ordinary awards show; it was hailed as the biggest party for kids on the planet and amidst all the excitement and celebration, Bindi's appearance held a special significance. It marked her first public appearance since her father's passing, showcasing her resilience and determination to carry on his legacy.

Bindi's presence on that stage was nothing short of awe-inspiring. Her poise and grace in such a challenging time captured hearts around the world. As she handed out the award with a smile that masked her grief, it became clear that Bindi possessed an inner strength beyond her years.

The energy in the room must have been electrifying as kids from all over Australia gathered to celebrate their favorite stars and enjoy an unforgettable night of fun.

The Nickelodeon Australian Kids Choice Awards has always been known for its vibrant atmosphere and exciting surprises. It is a true testament to how much joy and excitement can be created when children come together to honor their beloved celebrities.

So imagine yourself transported back in time to that magical evening in 2006, where Bindi Irwin stole hearts with her charm and grace. The Nickelodeon Australian Kids Choice Awards truly lived up to its reputation as the biggest party for kids on this remarkable planet we call home and it will forever be remembered as a platform where Bindi showcased her love for entertaining children.

Prepare to be amazed by the incredible journey of the multi talented Bindi Irwin in the world of music! Not only did she make a name for herself in the world of wildlife conservation, but she also embarked on a music career that left everyone in awe.

It all began on 27 November 2006, when this remarkable young talent released her debut album, "Bindi Kid Fitness," alongside her father, the legendary Steve Irwin, and The Crocmen. Can you imagine the excitement and anticipation surrounding such a collaboration?

But Bindi's musical prowess didn't stop there. Just a year later, on 17 November 2007, she took the world by storm with her very first single titled "Trouble in the Jungle." This catchy tune undoubtedly showcased Bindi's unique style and undeniable talent. "Trouble in the Jungle" includes a tribute song to her father Steve called "My Daddy The Crocodile Hunter".

But that's not all – Bindi showcased her musical prowess on The Today Show alongside The Crocmen in November 2007. With her captivating voice, she sang "Trouble in the Jungle," captivating audiences with her talent and infectious energy. Just imagine the energy and excitement they must have brought to the stage!

As if conquering the fitness world and mesmerizing

audiences on television wasn't enough, Bindi took it upon herself to learn how to play the piano. Talk about dedication and determination!

Bindi's ability to excel in various fields is truly awe-inspiring. From wildlife conservation to music and even mastering an instrument like the piano, there seems to be no limit to her talents. She is truly a remarkable individual!

On 11 October 2008, this extraordinary young talent released her second album, "Bindi Kid Fitness 2 Jungle Dance Party." Can you believe it? At such a young age, Bindi was already making waves with her infectious tunes.

And it doesn't stop there. Bindi's passion for music extended beyond albums. She also ventured into creating DVDs, sharing her love for dance and fitness with children all around the world. Her dedication to promoting a healthy lifestyle through joyful movement is truly awe-inspiring.

So let's take a moment to appreciate the incredible journey of Bindi – from her early days with "Bindi and The Crocmen" to releasing her own albums like "Bindi Kid Fitness 2 Jungle Dance Party" and spreading positivity through dance.

She also formed a sensational band in 2009 known as "Bindi and The Jungle Girls". Can you believe it? A young girl with a passion for music and adventure, ready to conquer the stage!

Fast forward to 2013, and Bindi was ready to take her musical prowess to new heights. She released her third album titled "Bindi and The Jungle Girls African Dance Party". Just imagine the rhythm and energy infused into each track, transporting listeners on a captivating journey through African beats and melodies.

But Bindi's musical journey didn't stop there. In 2016, she unleashed her fourth album upon the world – "Bindi and The Jungle Girls Bindi's Island Dance Party". Can you feel the excitement building up? This album surely promises an exhilarating experience filled with vibrant island vibes that will make you want to dance along.

Bindi's dedication to her music career is truly awe-inspiring. From forming her own band to releasing multiple albums showcasing different themes and genres, she has proven herself as not just an animal conservationist but also a talented musician. She has seamlessly transitioned from her conservation efforts to conquering the music industry.

Bindi also immersed us in her captivating sounds with her band "Bindi and The Jungle Girls", from their African Dance Party album in 2013 to their Island Dance Party release in 2016. Bindi is truly an extraordinary artist! Her dedication and passion shine through in every note she sings. It's very clear that she has left an indelible mark on the music industry and continues to inspire us all.

Later Bindi would appear on "The Ellen DeGeneres Show" January 11, 2007. While on the show in Los Angeles she told Ellen that she wanted to try to be like her 44-year father who had recently passed away. With Bindi commenting,"I feel like I'm him. I want him to be proud of me." She said while she appeared with her mom holding a lizard face to face.

In a heartwarming and courageous interview, Bindi shared her aspirations to follow in her father's footsteps and continue his remarkable legacy. Dressed in her father's iconic khaki attire, this eight-year-old powerhouse demonstrated an incredible passion for animals as she confidently introduced a blue-tongued lizard named Spanky. Bindi's appearance on the show not only showcased her natural charm but also marked the beginning of her own television career and her efforts to promote Australian tourism.

*Bindi Irwin with her mom Terri Irwin on the Ellen
DeGeneres Show (Photo credit: Ellen DeGeneres Show NBC
Studios)*

At just eight years old, Bindi had already proven herself to
be a natural in front of the cameras. Following in the footsteps
of her beloved father, Steve Irwin, she exudes confidence and
enthusiasm when it comes to interacting with wildlife. Her
devotion to animals was nurtured by Steve himself, who
instilled in her a deep love for nature from an early age. On
"The Ellen DeGeneres Show," Bindi proudly expressed how
much her dad influenced her passion for animals and inspired
her desire to follow in his extraordinary footsteps.

During her unforgettable interview on "The Ellen
DeGeneres Show," Bindi captivated both the host and
audience with her infectious energy and genuine love for
wildlife. Holding Spanky the blue-tongued lizard close to her
heart, she effortlessly engaged with Ellen while recounting

cherished memories of working alongside her dad. It was evident that Bindi inherited not only Steve's affinity for animals but also his ability to connect with people through their shared fascination with the natural world.

Bindi's appearance on the show was just the beginning of her exciting journey in the entertainment industry. As part of her efforts to promote Australian tourism, she is set to star in her own series, "Bindi, The Jungle Girl," which will be aired on the Discovery Kids network later this year. This new venture allows Bindi to combine her passion for wildlife conservation with her natural talent for captivating audiences young and old. With each step she takes, Bindi is carving out her own path while honoring her father's legacy.

The tragic loss of Steve Irwin shook the world, but it was his daughter who delivered a touching eulogy at his memorial service, demonstrating strength and wisdom beyond her years. Bindi continues to carry her father's memory close to her heart as she embarks on this incredible journey. Her determination to make him proud is evident in every endeavor she undertakes. Through television appearances, wildlife advocacy, and heartfelt speeches, Bindi strives to ensure that Steve's love for animals lives on through everything she does.

As we witness Bindi's remarkable journey unfold before our eyes, it becomes clear that she possesses not only an undeniable talent but also an unwavering dedication to creating positive change in the world of wildlife conservation. From appearing on "The Ellen DeGeneres Show" to starring in her own television series, Bindi was well on her way to becoming a force to be reckoned with. She serves as an inspiration not only to young aspiring conservationists but also adults who are moved by her genuine commitment and courage.

Bindi's appearance on "The Ellen DeGeneres Show" showcased a young girl determined to honor her father's legacy by making a difference in the world of wildlife conservation. Her infectious enthusiasm and genuine love for animals captivated both Ellen and the audience, leaving a lasting impression. As Bindi's journey unfolds, we eagerly anticipate the positive impact she will continue to make in her efforts to preserve and protect our precious natural world.

Welcome to another trip down memory lane as we revisit one of the most unforgettable moments in television history. It was back in January 16, 2007 when a nine-year-old Bindi graced the American morning news show "Today" with her presence. Little did anyone know that this pint-sized wildlife enthusiast would leave an indelible mark with her passionate performance – a rap song about endangered species. Bindi's appearance on the show left a lasting impact on both young Bindi's career and our collective consciousness.

Bindi Irwin on the Today Show (Photo credit: MSNBC The Today Show)

As the cameras rolled and millions of viewers tuned in to watch their usual morning news fix, they were in for a delightful surprise. Bindi, already following in her father's footsteps as an advocate for wildlife conservation, took center stage with an unexpected musical performance. With youthful exuberance and an earnest desire to raise awareness about endangered species, she delivered a rap with a purpose that captured hearts across the nation.

Bindi's rap showcased her passion for wildlife preservation while educating audiences about the plight of endangered species. Even though some might describe it as slightly awkward due to her tender age at the time, there was no denying the sincerity behind her words. As she rapped about animals facing extinction, she highlighted their unique qualities and emphasized the importance of taking action to protect them while shedding light on endangered Species.

In one verse of her memorable rap, Bindi drew attention to specific endangered animals such as tigers and elephants, shedding light on their dwindling populations due to habitat loss and poaching. Her infectious enthusiasm coupled with educational lyrics made for a captivating performance that left viewers both entertained and informed.

Bindi's appearance on the "Today" show was more than just a charming television moment. It served as a catalyst, inspiring young minds to get involved in conservation efforts and make a difference in the world. Her passion and dedication resonated with children and adults alike, showing that age should never be a barrier when it comes to advocating for causes we believe in.

The impact of Bindi's rap performance extended far beyond that single morning on the "Today" show. It also ignited conversations about wildlife conservation, raising awareness and prompting individuals to reflect on their own role in protecting endangered species for a new generation of Conservationists.

For many viewers, young and old, Bindi became an inspiration. Her unwavering commitment to wildlife preservation encouraged countless individuals to become actively involved in conservation efforts themselves. Whether it was through supporting organizations focused on protecting endangered species or making lifestyle changes to reduce their ecological footprint, Bindi's rap had a lasting impact.

Bindi's rap not only left an impression on audiences worldwide but also solidified her own place as an advocate for wildlife conservation. Since that iconic performance, she has continued to carry her father's legacy forward by dedicating her life to preserving our planet's biodiversity and educating others about the importance of coexisting with nature.

Sometimes, it's those unexpected moments that stick with us the most – moments like Bindi Irwin rapping about endangered species on the "Today" show. This unforgettable performance not only captivated audiences but also sparked conversations and inspired action.

As we look back at this remarkable event, let us remember the power of youth advocacy, the importance of conserving our planet's precious creatures, and how one small act can leave a lasting impact. May we all find inspiration from Bindi's passionate rap about endangered species and strive to make a positive difference in the world around us.

The Late Show with David Letterman has played host to countless iconic figures over the years, but few have left such a lasting impression as young Bindi Irwin did January 16, 2007 while Bindi and her Mom promoted Australia Week 2007. The audience was immediately enthralled by her boundless energy and infectious charm.

During her appearance on the Late Show, Bindi proudly fulfilled her duties as a newly appointed "tourism ambassador" for Australia. With her radiant smile and undeniable passion for wildlife conservation, she effortlessly showcased the natural wonders and unique experiences that Australia has to offer. Through her vibrant personality and engaging storytelling, Bindi inspired viewers to embark on their own adventures Down Under.

In addition to being an advocate for wildlife conservation, Bindi used her platform on the Late Show to promote her new video series: Bindi Kid Fitness. This innovative project aimed to encourage children around the world to stay active and embrace a healthy lifestyle by incorporating fun exercises into their daily routines. With her characteristic exuberance, Bindi demonstrated various fitness routines that were both entertaining and accessible to young viewers.

Beyond her promotional endeavors, Bindi provided a glimpse into her life during her interview with David Letterman. She shared that creative writing was her favorite subject, allowing her to express her love for animals through storytelling. However, she admitted that math was not her strong suit, a sentiment many viewers could likely relate to. Bindi also expressed her enjoyment of being homeschooled, highlighting the unique bond she shared with her teachers who doubled as cherished friends.

Bindi Irwin's appearance on the Late Show with David Letterman in 2007 left an indelible mark on audiences worldwide. Her infectious personality and unwavering dedication to wildlife conservation continue to inspire individuals of all ages to this day. Through her advocacy work and promotion of Bindi Kid Fitness, she has encouraged countless children to embrace their passion for animals while prioritizing their physical well-being.

Bindi's appearance on the Late Show with David Letterman in 2007 showcased not only her remarkable charisma but also her commitment to making a positive impact on the world. From promoting Australia as a tourism ambassador to encouraging kids to stay active through Bindi Kid Fitness, Bindi demonstrated that age is no barrier when it comes to inspiring others. Her legacy serves as a reminder that even the youngest voices can create significant change and leave an enduring impression on global audiences.

Prepare to be amazed by the star-studded event that took place on March 31, 2007! The 20th Annual Nickelodeon Kids Choice Awards in Los Angeles was a night filled with excitement and unforgettable moments. One of the highlights of the evening was when the talented Bindi Irwin, alongside George Lopez and Tyler James Williams, took to the stage to present an award.

Terri and Bindi Irwin at the 20th Annual Nickelodeon Kids Choice Awards in Los Angeles, California (Photo credit: PictureLux/The Hollywood Archive)

The anticipation reached its peak as Bindi Irwin stepped forward to announce the winner of "Favorite Male Singer." The crowd held their breath as she revealed that none other than Justin Timberlake had won this prestigious accolade. Can you imagine being in Bindi's shoes at such a young age? It must have been absolutely thrilling!

The energy in Pauley Pavilion at the University of California soared as Justin Timberlake accepted his award that was accompanied by a thunderous applause.

It's truly awe-inspiring how these young stars came together for this memorable occasion. Bindi Irwin's presence added an extra touch of elegance and charm to an already star-studded event. And let's not forget that Justin Timberlake himself was not only a winner but also had the honor of hosting this incredible show.

But wait... there's more! The Nickelodeon Kids Choice Awards is famous for its tradition of drenching celebrities in green goo. And let me tell you, that night was no exception. I can only imagine the laughter and surprise as everyone watched Justin Timberlake get covered in that slimy green substance. Talk about an unforgettable moment!

The 20th Annual Nickelodeon Kids Choice Awards truly captured the essence of fun and excitement with Bindi Irwin's presence, Justin Timberlake's well-deserved win, and of course, the signature green goo tradition. It's moments like these that make us appreciate just how incredible award shows can be.

This momentous occasion serves as a testament to the power and influence of these remarkable individuals in shaping popular culture. It is a reminder that even at such a young age, they were able to captivate audiences worldwide with their talent and charisma.

So let us take a moment to reflect on this extraordinary event where Bindi Irwin shared her radiance alongside George Lopez and Tyler James Williams, presenting Justin Timberlake with his well-deserved award for "Favorite Male Singer" at the 20th Annual Nickelodeon Kids Choice Awards in Los Angeles. I don't know about you, but I'm feeling absolutely awestruck by this incredible evening!

In the vibrant world of Australian television, May 6, 2007 was a remarkable year, filled with captivating performances and memorable moments. One such moment that stole the limelight was when Bindi, alongside the talented comedian Glenn Robbins, graced the stage to present an award at the prestigious TV Logie Awards. The 49th Annual TV Week Logie Awards was held on Sunday 6 May 2007 at the Crown Palladium in Melbourne, and broadcast on the Nine Network.

Before we delve into Bindi Irwin's role at the Logie Awards, let's set the stage by exploring what this illustrious event represents. The Logie Awards are Australia's most esteemed television awards ceremony, celebrating excellence across various genres and categories. It serves as a platform to recognize outstanding talent and productions that have captivated audiences throughout the year.

Television personalities, industry professionals, and fans eagerly anticipate this star-studded affair each year. It is an evening filled with anticipation, laughter, tears, and celebration as deserving individuals are acknowledged for their contributions to Australian television.

One particular highlight of the May 6, 2007 Logie Awards was when Bindi Irwin took center stage alongside renowned comedian Glenn Robbins. Together, they had the honor of presenting the award for "Most Outstanding Children's Show." This category recognizes exceptional programs designed specifically for young viewers that entertain while also educating or inspiring them.

The atmosphere crackled with excitement as Bindi and Glenn stepped up to announce the nominees and reveal who would be taking home this prestigious accolade. The audience held its breath in anticipation as they eagerly awaited their opening lines and infectious charm.

With grace and poise beyond her years, Bindi Irwin announced the winner of the "Most Outstanding Children's Show" category – The Upside Down Show. This whimsical and imaginative program had captured the hearts of children and adults alike with its clever storytelling, interactive elements, and captivating performances.

As Bindi revealed the recipient of this coveted award, cheers erupted in the crowd. The Upside Down Show team took to the stage, beaming with pride and gratitude, as they accepted their Logie Award. It was a moment of triumph for the creators, cast, and crew who had poured their hearts into crafting a show that resonated with young audiences across Australia.

Bindi's presence at the Logie Awards was not only a testament to her status as a beloved figure but also marked her emergence as an influential force in Australian entertainment. At such a young age, she effortlessly commanded attention on stage alongside comedy veteran Glenn Robbins.

This memorable night showcased Bindi's ability to captivate audiences with her genuine charisma, infectious enthusiasm, and deep passion for wildlife conservation – qualities that would continue to define her journey in the years to come. It was clear that Bindi Irwin was destined for greatness in her own right.

As we look back on 2007's Logie Awards, it is impossible to overlook the impact of Bindi Irwin's involvement. Her collaboration with Glenn Robbins in presenting the award for "Most Outstanding Children's Show" added an extra sparkle to an already enchanting evening.

Bindi's poised presence on stage showcased her maturity and talent beyond her years. As she celebrated excellence in children's programming alongside industry veterans, it became evident that she was carving out her own path as an influential figure in entertainment.

The TV Week Logie Awards of 2007 will forever be etched in our memories as the night Bindi Irwin shone brightly and celebrated the magic of Australian television. Her award-winning moment marked not only a milestone in her career but also symbolized the beginning of a journey that would see her inspire millions around the world.

Australia, known for its stunning landscapes, unique wildlife, and vibrant culture, has always been a top destination for travelers around the world. When it comes to promoting Australian tourism, one name stands out above the rest, Bindi. The pint-sized entertainer and wildlife warrior was crowned the favorite face of Australian tourism May 16, 2007 while she was visiting the U.S.A.

Bindi was the perfect natural born ambassador for Australian tourism because her passion for environmental conservation has captured the hearts of both locals and international visitors. With 38 percent of the votes, Bindi emerged as the clear winner in the survey conducted over five weeks by online travel directory TotalTravel.com. 1,609 participants were asked who they thought was the best ambassador for the industry.

Bindi became the clear winner with 38% voting for her as the Queen of Australian tourism. Prince of the portaloos scored 28% of the votes, while foxy Morin's Kath and Kim came in third place with 24% of the votes.

Shane Warne, a retired cricketer, scored only 6% of the votes, while Bert Newton got the least votes with only 5%. After all the votes were tallied up Total travel.com global marketing Manager Paul Fisher commented he was not surprised in the least bit that Bindi had topped the poll because he believed in the beginning she would be a "perfect ambassador " for Australia.

With Paul commenting,"Australians think that she's a fresh face, very genuine. She's obviously associated with all the good things I guess to do with the Australian environment. She's certainly a very lively and likable character as well. The Australian people have fallen in love with a very bright, talented and well adjusted young girl, who, like her late father, is passionate about the environment and conservation."

"I am sure international visitors would love to see Bindi say 'G'day mate." Bailey also commented that Bindi would not replace bikini model Laura Bengal as Australia's official in any overseas television advertising."

But Federal Tourism Minister Fran Bailey said it was probably not appropriate for Bindi to be the face of the Australian industry seeing she is only a child. Bailey would later comment, "There is no role for Bindi in any advertising campaign." "The role that an ambassador is called upon really calls for an adult person in those roles, but we are absolutely delighted to be able to be blessed to have Bindi coming along with her mum to a lot of our major tourism events."

So at the ripe age of eight years old Bindi received the award, while she had already captivated audiences with her infectious energy and genuine love for Australia's rich biodiversity. As the daughter of the late Steve Irwin, Bindi continued to carry on her father's legacy as a wildlife advocate and conservationist. Her dedication to preserving Australia's unique flora and fauna made her an ideal ambassador for promoting eco-tourism in the country.

Bindi's connection to Australia's natural wonders runs deep. While she grew up at Australia Zoo she developed a profound appreciation for wildlife from an early age. Like her father, she possesses an innate ability to connect with animals and shares their stories with enthusiasm. Through various television programs and public appearances, Bindi showcases Australia's diverse ecosystems and educates viewers about the importance of conservation efforts.

One of the reasons why Bindi received overwhelming support in the survey is her genuine passion for environmental conservation. Whether it's raising awareness about endangered species or advocating for sustainable practices, she consistently emphasizes our duty to protect nature. By highlighting Australia's unique wildlife and fragile ecosystems, Bindi encourages visitors to experience the country's natural beauty while fostering a sense of responsibility towards its preservation while making her a role model for the young and the old.

Bindi's appeal extends beyond her young age. While she captures the hearts of children, her message resonates with people of all generations. Her commitment to wildlife conservation inspires individuals to take action in their own lives and make a positive impact on the environment. Bindi's infectious enthusiasm and warm personality create an instant connection with people from all walks of life, making her an influential figure in promoting Australian tourism which made Australia proud.

As TotalTravel.com's global marketing manager, Paul Fisher, rightly pointed out, Bindi Irwin is a "perfect ambassador" for Australia. Her infectious love for her country, combined with her passion for environmental conservation, makes her an ideal representative of Australian tourism. International visitors are eager to experience Australia through the eyes of Bindi, as she embodies the spirit of the nation with her bright smile and genuine warmth.

With her victory as the queen of Australian tourism, Bindi solidifies herself as a beloved figure not just in Australia but around the world. Her unwavering dedication to wildlife conservation and infectious personality make her an exceptional ambassador for promoting Australian tourism. Through Bindi's efforts, visitors are not only drawn to Australia's stunning landscapes but also inspired to protect its precious ecosystems. As we continue to witness Bindi's impact on both locals and international travelers alike, it is clear that she will reign as the queen of Aussie tourism for years to come.

4

CHAPTER 4

———————

Then on Friday, June 8, 2007, a one-hour U.S. television documentary film aired on Animal Planet that captured the hearts of viewers worldwide. Titled "My Daddy the Crocodile Hunter," this poignant film served as both a memorial for the legendary conservationist Steve Irwin and a glimpse into the life of his remarkable daughter, Bindi. Now let us delve into the touching moments and behind-the-scenes footage that made this documentary an unforgettable tribute to Steve's legacy.

Bindi Irwin in My Daddy the Crocodile Hunter (Photo credit: Animal Planet)

Bindi carried on the legacy of her father during the documentary by taking the viewers behind the scenes, on a very private and personal look at what it was like growing up with her famous dad in the Outback of Australia.

Quickly Bindi started following in her father's footsteps as an animal and nature lover as she carried on his legacy. Within the show you see rare home movies of Bindi's birth, her early childhood and some behind the scenes on- location shots of her father's most thrilling and exciting TV shows and movies.

At just nine years old, Bindi took center stage in "My Daddy the Crocodile Hunter." With grace and maturity beyond her tender age, Bindi guided viewers through her unique upbringing alongside her beloved father in the vast outback of Australia. This intimate look provided an insight into what it truly meant to grow up as Steve Irwin's daughter while the film also served as a memorial for her father.

The film showcased rare home movies capturing precious moments from Bindi's birth and early childhood. These heartwarming scenes painted a picture of a family deeply rooted in their love for animals and nature. We witnessed how Steve's passion for wildlife not only shaped his own life but also passed down to his young daughter. The documentary also served as an introduction to Bindi's new TV Series, Bindi the Jungle Girl. The aim of filming the 26-part cable TV show was to get children more interested in wildlife conservation.

As the film unfolded, audiences were treated to exclusive behind-the-scenes footage of some of Steve Irwin's most thrilling adventures. From daring encounters with crocodiles to exhilarating TV shows and movies shot on location, viewers were captivated by his unwavering dedication to wildlife conservation.

One particularly poignant moment was when Bindi joined her father on his last crocodile research adventure in August 2006. The footage showcased their shared enthusiasm as they fearlessly captured crocodiles together—a testament to Steve's legacy being carried forward by his courageous daughter.

While "My Daddy the Crocodile Hunter" paid tribute to Steve, it also served as an introduction to Bindi's own television series, "Bindi the Jungle Girl." This 26-part cable TV show aimed to ignite children's interest in wildlife conservation and foster a deeper connection with the natural world.

Through her new series, Bindi continued her father's legacy by inspiring young minds to appreciate and protect the wonders of nature. By sharing her own adventures and experiences, she encouraged children to become active participants in conservation efforts, just like her dad had done throughout his life.

"My Daddy the Crocodile Hunter" left an indelible mark on viewers worldwide. It showcased the deep bond between a father and daughter, illustrating how love for animals can unite generations. The film not only celebrated Steve's extraordinary life but also highlighted Bindi's determination to carry forward his mission of wildlife preservation.

The remarkable journey shared in this film serves as a timeless reminder that passion knows no boundaries and that love for our natural world can be nurtured from a young age. Through their inspiring story, both Steve and Bindi have forever etched their names in the annals of wildlife conservation.

As we reminisce about this heartfelt tribute on Animal Planet, let us remember the enduring legacy of Steve Irwin—a man who touched countless lives—and celebrate Bindi's unwavering commitment to protecting our planet for future generations.

While Bindi was rising to stardom at such a young age critics in Australia and in other parts of the world accused Terri and her advisors of trying to rush Bindi into the show business limelight when she's way too young to cope with the celebrity life. However Bindi was never pressured by her family to do anything she did not want to do.

Bindi would later carve her own path in the world of wildlife conservation and television. On June 9, 2007, she burst onto the Australian television scene with her own show, "Bindi the Jungle Girl." Over 26 episodes that ran into 2008, Bindi captivated audiences with her infectious enthusiasm for animals and her unique approach to showcasing wildlife. However, this show also sparked controversy due to its use of footage featuring Bindi's father, leading to mixed reactions from critics and viewers alike.

Bindi Irwin in The Jungle Girl (Photo credit Discovery Kids and the Australian Broadcasting Corporation)

"Bindi the Jungle Girl" followed a distinctive format that combined fresh footage of Bindi exploring wildlife with older clips featuring her beloved father, Steve Irwin. The seamless interweaving of these two elements created an enchanting viewing experience that showcased both Bindi's present-day adventures and paid homage to her father's legacy. From their tree house nestled high up in the rainforest, Bindi introduced viewers to a captivating world of animals while occasionally being joined by her parents who shared their own animal tales.

While many viewers were thrilled to see Steve Irwin on

screen once again through archival footage, others found it unsettling. Critics labeled the show as "creepy" and expressed a sense of unease at witnessing Steve's presence despite his untimely passing. To some extent, it felt as though he was alive within the show without any acknowledgement of his passing. This polarizing aspect generated heated discussions among television critics and the general public, with opinions ranging from admiration for the tribute to Steve Irwin to discomfort at the blurring of reality and fiction.

As Bindi rose to stardom at a young age, concerns were raised about her being thrust into the spotlight too soon. Critics in Australia and around the world accused Terri Irwin, Bindi's mother, and her advisors of pushing her into show business prematurely. They argued that she was too young to handle the pressures of fame and the demands of celebrity life. However, it is important to note that Bindi was never forced or pressured by her family to pursue a career in television or wildlife conservation. Her passion for animals shone through naturally, and her involvement in "Bindi the Jungle Girl" stemmed from genuine interest and enthusiasm.

Throughout "Bindi the Jungle Girl," it became evident that Bindi's love for wildlife was both genuine and infectious. Her interactions with various creatures showcased not only her knowledge but also her deep empathy and respect for all living beings. Whether she was cuddling a koala or swimming alongside sea turtles, Bindi's enthusiasm emanated from every frame. Her ability to engage viewers of all ages and inspire them to appreciate nature played a significant role in the show's success.

"Bindi the Jungle Girl" served as a crucial stepping stone in Bindi Irwin's journey towards becoming an influential figure in wildlife conservation. The show helped solidify her position as an advocate for animal rights and environmental preservation, amplifying her voice on a global scale. While controversy surrounded aspects of the show, there is no denying its impact in shaping Bindi's trajectory as an individual dedicated to continuing her father's legacy while forging her own path.

"Bindi the Jungle Girl" stands as a testament to Bindi's remarkable passion for wildlife and her commitment to spreading awareness about conservation. Despite the controversy surrounding the inclusion of Steve Irwin in the show, Bindi's infectious energy and genuine love for animals captured the hearts of viewers around the world. From her tree house in the rainforest, she brought joy, education, and a sense of wonder into countless homes. "Bindi the Jungle Girl" not only showcased Bindi's incredible potential but also served as a platform that propelled her towards becoming an influential force in wildlife conservation.

On June 13, 2007 an extraordinary meeting took place at the Australia Zoo that captured the attention and hearts of thousands of people. Bindi Irwin, the passionate wildlife conservationist had the honor of meeting Your Holiness The 14th Dalai Lama for a koala rendezvous at the Australia Zoo. This momentous occasion unfolded in front of a crowd of 5,000 individuals at the iconic "Crocoseum," where both Bindi and His Holiness spoke about kindness towards animals and the environment. Let us dive into this remarkable encounter that brought together two influential figures to shed light on compassion and love for all living beings.

The Dalai Lama, right, poses with the Irwin family, Bindi, center holding Koala, Bob, lower left, and mother Terry, left, at Australia Zoo in Beerwah, Australia, Wednesday June 13, 2007. (AP Photo/Steve Holland)

The Australia Zoo was buzzing with excitement as Bindi Irwin stood alongside Your Holiness The 14th Dalai Lama. It was a poignant moment, symbolizing unity between humans and nature. Both individuals share a deep passion for animal welfare, making their rendezvous even more meaningful.

As His Holiness toured The Australian Zoo, he took a moment to express his gratitude towards the Irwin family's unwavering dedication to wildlife conservation. Their tireless efforts in protecting and preserving endangered species have not gone unnoticed by one of the world's most revered spiritual leaders.

During this memorable visit, Your Holiness The 14th Dalai Lama did more than simply admire the animals at the Crocoseum; he also launched Kindness Week – an initiative aimed at promoting compassion and empathy towards all beings. From his platform atop that grand stage, he addressed thousands of eager listeners for over thirty minutes.

The words spoken by His Holiness resonated deeply within each heart present in that crowd. He emphasized how taking care of animals is not only crucial for their well-being but also essential for cultivating happiness among human beings. As the Dalai Lama delivered his message, Buddhist prayer flags gently swayed in the breeze, symbolizing unity and reverence for life.

His Holiness The 14th Dalai Lama, drawing from his own experiences, shared anecdotes of his youth growing up in Tibet. He spoke of how he would rescue animals from slaughterhouses, displaying his profound empathy towards all creatures. With conviction in his voice, he addressed the cruelty that exists within the world today: "Hunting, beef, sheep farms, piggeries – millions, billions die. We can be so cruel to animals."

The Dalai Lama did not shy away from criticizing organizations and companies that remain indifferent to animal rights by subjecting them to unethical experimentation. His words carried weight as he urged everyone to embrace a more compassionate lifestyle – one that involves consuming less meat and increasing vegetable consumption. In doing so, he believed that humanity could restore its lost sense of compassion.

During his address at the Crocoseum, His Holiness The 14th Dalai Lama spoke candidly about his personal journey towards vegetarianism. In 1965, he made a conscious decision to become egg, dairy, and meat-free. While admitting occasional lapses in adherence to this diet himself, he extolled the benefits of embracing vegetarianism as a way to show respect and kindness towards animals.

By sharing his own choices and encouraging others to consider a plant-based diet, the Dalai Lama highlighted the interconnectedness between our dietary preferences and our capacity for compassion. It was a call for individuals to reflect on their daily choices and recognize how they can contribute positively towards creating a more harmonious world.

He also criticized organizations and companies that continue to "remain indifferent " to animal rights by experimenting on them. While he also encouraged everyone to eat more vegetables and not so much meat, claiming the world lacked compassion because there was too much extremism.

As His Holiness concluded his inspiring speech at the Australia Zoo's Crocoseum, he left everyone with a thought-provoking statement: "Most troublemakers on this planet, so-called terrorists, if you investigate their whole life, particularly at the time of childhood, I think there is something lacking." It was a call for society to reflect on how we raise our children and the values we instill in them.

The Dalia Lama also spoke about the importance of family while he urged parents to show their children as much compassion as possible while he suggested that children be taught "warmheartedness" as part of school curriculum. While he admitted laughing to everyone, "I'm a monk, so I have no children.....but I may lose my temper."

The Dalia Lama's visit ended shortly after Terri, Bindi and Robert came on the stage of the stage of Crocoseum with Bindi clutching in her arms a Koala and The Dalia Lama saying," He is rather lazy ....just like myself," as The Dalia Lama joked about the Koala nestled in Bindi's arms he presented the Irwin family with Buddhist white scarves, or katas, which are used to signal the positive start of new relationships.

Tickets to the event sold out within two days after going

on sale. The event attracted not only friends and family of the Irwin's, but also Queensland Former Governor Quentin Bryce.

As we reflect on the extraordinary encounter between Bindi Irwin and Your Holiness The 14th Dalai Lama at the Australia Zoo, we are reminded of the power of love, compassion, and unity. This meeting showcased two influential figures who have dedicated their lives to making a difference in our world – one through her unwavering commitment to wildlife conservation and education, and the other through his teachings of kindness and mindfulness.

The powerful words spoken by Your Holiness The 14th Dalai Lama during his visit to the Australia Zoo not only touched upon animal welfare but also challenged us to examine our own actions and choices. Through his wisdom and unwavering commitment to compassion, he left an indelible mark on all those fortunate enough to witness this historic rendezvous. May this meeting serve as a reminder of the importance of kindness towards animals and inspire us all to make a positive impact in the world around us.

In these challenging times, it is more crucial than ever that we extend empathy not only towards each other but also towards all living beings that share our planet. Let us take inspiration from this remarkable rendezvous and strive to cultivate kindness in our daily lives. Together, we can create a more compassionate world where both humans and animals can thrive harmoniously.

Bindi would later launch her own line of children's clothing while walking the catwalk at the MAGIC trade show in Las Vega, Nevada on August 29, 2007, with a python draped around her shoulders at her fashion show which featured her clothing line called Bindi Wear International, featuring safari – style separates.

In the world of fashion, it's not uncommon to come across celebrities who launch their own clothing lines. But when Bindi Irwin, the daughter of the late Crocodile Hunter, Steve Irwin, stepped onto the catwalk at the MAGIC trade show in Las Vegas with a python draped around her shoulders, it was clear that her clothing line was going to be something truly unique and impactful.

Bindi Irwin on the Catwalk at the MAGIC trade show in Las Vegas (Photo credit: Getty Images)

Bindi took a leap of faith and ventured into the world of fashion while her goal was to create a line of children's clothing that not only made little ones look adorable, but also spread awareness about pressing environmental issues.

The idea for Bindi Wear International originated at the Australia Zoo, where a family friend named Mr. Palmina DiStasi designed apparel for newborns up to thirteen-year-olds. With Bindi's input and artwork, he crafted safari-style separates that embodied her passion for wildlife conservation with one hundred percent of the proceeds going towards supporting the Australia Zoo's conservation programs.

Bindi Wear International quickly gained attention for its unique approach to children's fashion. Each garment featured messages handwritten by Bindi herself, aimed at educating young people about environmental concerns such as deforestation and animal consumption. The brand became synonymous with "clothing with a conscience," while it encouraged kids worldwide to join in promoting wildlife conservation that was aimed towards building awareness to young people all over the world about the environment and to help promote conservation of wildlife while helping the Australia Zoo spread its message through fashion.

Not only did this clothing line capture hearts with its meaningful designs, but it also operated on a noble mission. One hundred percent of the proceeds from Bindi Wear International went towards supporting the Australia Zoo's conservation programs. By purchasing an item from Bindi's collection, parents were not only dressing their children in stylish outfits but also contributing to the preservation of wildlife.

Bindi Wear International's spring/summer collections showcased a range of captivating themes, each with its own message and purpose. Let's take a closer look at some of these inspiring themes that captivated both children and adults alike:

1. Green is the New Black – Promoting Koala Conservation

The first theme, "Green is the New Black," focused on raising awareness about koala conservation. Featuring vibrant green hues and adorable koala prints, this collection aimed to educate young minds about the importance of preserving these iconic Australian creatures.

2. Jungle Safari – Embracing Crocodile Camouflage

In the "Jungle Safari" theme, Bindi Wear International took inspiration from crocodile camouflage prints. This adventurous collection aimed to instill a sense of wonder in children while teaching them about the beauty and diversity of wildlife found in jungles around the world.

3. Baby Warrior – Fun Animal Prints for Little Ones

"Baby Warrior" was a delightful theme designed specifically for babies. With playful animal prints adorning onesies and tiny t-shirts, this collection encouraged even the youngest members of society to become warriors for the environment.

4. Punk Warrior – Protecting Animals and the Environment

The "Punk Warrior" theme empowered older children to become protectors of animals and the environment. Combining edgy designs with powerful messages, this collection inspired kids to stand up for what they believe in and make a difference.

5. Industrial Cowgirl and Cowboy – Celebrating Nature Enhanced by Technology

The final theme, "Industrial Cowgirl and Cowboy," celebrated mankind's ability to coexist harmoniously with nature through technological advancements. This collection showcased the fusion of traditional Western elements with modern design, reminding us that progress and conservation can go hand in hand.

Bindi Wear International went beyond just clothing; it offered an entire world of stylish options for children. The brand featured a variety of casual daywear, including t-shirts, cargos, hoodies, and dresses. But Bindi didn't stop there – she expanded her line to include bags, footwear, sleepwear, hats, and swimwear.

With prices ranging from $10 to $40 dollars at wholesale, Bindi made sure her clothing was accessible to families who wanted to make a difference while dressing their little ones in style where fashion met Conservation.

Bindi's journey from receiving an award to launching her own line of children's clothing is truly remarkable. Through Bindi Wear International, she not only created fashionable garments but also used her platform to educate young minds about environmental issues and promote wildlife conservation. By combining her passion for fashion with her dedication to preserving nature, Bindi became a true icon in the world of conservationist fashion. So why should you buy a Goldendoodle? Well, they are intelligent animals with friendly and trainable nature which are similar traits found in Bindi herself. Just like Bindi's clothing line stood out among the rest by combining style with purpose, Goldendoodles stand out among dog breeds as loyal companions that bring joy and happiness into our lives.

Nickelodeon's Australian Kids Choice Awards is a star-studded event that brings together the best of Australia's entertainment industry while giving kids the power to choose their favorites. In a delightful twist on October 10, 2007, Bindi took center stage as she was awarded not one, but two prestigious accolades with the show hosted by the Veronicas and Zach Efron .

On that special day the Sydney Entertainment Center came alive with vibrant colors, laughter, and excitement as Nickelodeon hosted its annual Australian Kids Choice Awards. This highly anticipated event captivates audiences with its unique blend of entertainment and slime-filled surprises. The awards ceremony is famous for drenching celebrities in green goo, a tradition that adds an element of fun and unpredictability to the night.

In recognition of her outstanding contributions to conservation and her infectious passion for wildlife, Bindi was honored with the coveted "Fave Aussie" award. Voted on by her peers, this top accolade signifies not only Bindi's talent but also her impact on young minds around the world. Through her TV appearances, books, and unwavering commitment to carrying on her father's legacy, Bindi has become an inspiration for generations to come.

The second award bestowed upon Bindi was the "Biggest Greene" award. This recognition acknowledges her tireless efforts in upholding her father's work in conservation and animal welfare alongside her mother Terri. With boundless energy and unwavering dedication, Bindi has embraced her role as an advocate for wildlife and the environment, raising awareness about the importance of preserving our natural world.

Nickelodeon's Australian Kids Choice Awards is more than just an award show; it's a celebration of children's voices. With over 1 million votes cast through online and television platforms across 18 categories, this event empowers kids to make their voices heard. By honoring their favorite stars and entertainers, Nickelodeon reinforces the importance of individuality and showcases the impact that young people can have in shaping popular culture.

Bindi's recognition at Nickelodeon's Australian Kids Choice Awards is a testament to her unwavering passion, dedication, and positive influence on young minds worldwide. Her commitment to conservation and animal welfare has sparked a movement that transcends generations. Bindi's infectious enthusiasm reminds us all of the power we hold as individuals to make a difference in our world.

As time went by Bindi started to make a name for herself in the world of fitness and music and in November of 2007, she released two fitness DVDs for children and showcased her musical talent by performing "Trouble in the Jungle" on The Today Show with The Crocmen. This marked the beginning of her musical journey, which led to the release of her second album, Bindi Kid Fitness 2 Jungle Dance Party, on October 11th, 2008.

Bindi is not only passionate about wildlife conservation but also about promoting a healthy lifestyle among children. To encourage physical activity and fun exercise routines among young ones, she released two fitness DVDs specifically designed for children. Let's explore these energetic workouts:

DVD 1: Fitness Fun – Get Your Body Moving!

This DVD is perfect for kids who want to get their bodies moving while having a blast! It features a variety of exercises that are not only fun but also promote strength, flexibility, and coordination. From dance routines to animal-inspired movements, Bindi leads children through engaging workouts that make exercising an enjoyable experience.

DVD 2: Adventure Fit – Explore the Outdoors!

In this exciting DVD adventure, Bindi takes children on a journey through nature while incorporating fitness activities along the way. Kids can join her as they explore different environments and learn about animals while participating in adventurous exercises. Adventure Fit encourages outdoor play and teaches children how to stay active while appreciating the wonders of nature.

Bindi's fitness DVDs provide an excellent opportunity for children to engage in physical activity in an entertaining manner. By combining exercise and education about wildlife, she helps children develop a love for movement and a deeper connection with the natural world.

In addition to her fitness DVDs, Bindi Irwin displayed her musical talents during a captivating performance of "Trouble in the Jungle" on The Today Show. This lively song, performed alongside The Crocmen, showcased her growing skills as both a singer and performer. The audience was enthralled by Bindi's stage presence and infectious energy as she sang about the adventures and challenges one may encounter in the jungle.

"Trouble in the Jungle" not only entertained viewers but also served as a testament to Bindi's ability to captivate an audience with her musical talent. Her performance demonstrated that she was not just following in her father's footsteps in wildlife conservation but was also carving her own path in the world of music.

Following her successful performance on The Today Show, Bindi continued to pursue music and released her second album, Bindi Kid Fitness 2 Jungle Dance Party. This album showcased her growth as a musician and featured catchy tunes that motivated children to get up and dance while staying active.

With songs like "Jungle Dance," "Animal Communication," and "Rainforest Rumble," Bindi created an engaging musical experience that encouraged young listeners to move their bodies. Her ability to blend educational messages about wildlife with upbeat rhythms made this album both entertaining and informative.

Bindi's evolution as a musician proved that she had more than one talent up her sleeve. Through her music, she not only inspired children to stay fit but also imparted knowledge about nature and animal conservation, carrying on her family's legacy of environmental advocacy.

Bindi's journey into fitness DVDs for children and her foray into the world of music with "Trouble in the Jungle" and Bindi Kid Fitness 2 Jungle Dance Party demonstrate her multifaceted talent. Her dedication to promoting a healthy lifestyle among children, combined with her musical prowess, has made her a respected figure in both realms. Whether through engaging exercise routines or lively performances, Bindi's contributions continue to inspire young minds and encourage them to embrace an active lifestyle while nurturing a love for wildlife and music.

5

CHAPTER 5

Bindi's father Steve Irwin would later have a day started by the Australia Zoo in 2007 in his honor called Steve Irwin Day that comes around every year on November 15th. It is an annual International event honoring The Life and Legacy of Steve.

Every November 15th, the world comes together to celebrate Steve Irwin Day, a momentous occasion that pays tribute to the incredible life and legacy of Australia's beloved zookeeper, Steve Irwin. With his infectious enthusiasm, unwavering passion for wildlife, and larger-than-life personality, Steve captured the hearts of millions around the globe. Steve Irwin Day honors an extraordinary man who dedicated his life to conservation and spreading awareness about our precious natural world.

Steve Irwin (Photo credit The Irwin Family Australia Zoo)

To truly understand Steve's deep connection with animals, we must go back to his early years. Born on February 22, 1960, into a family with an insatiable love for wildlife, Steve was destined to become a champion for animals. His father was a renowned herpetologist and wildlife expert, while his mother devoted herself to rehabilitating injured or orphaned creatures. Growing up in this animal-filled home laid the foundation for Steve's lifelong dedication to protecting and conserving wildlife.

In 1970, when Steve was just ten years old, his family relocated to Queensland where they established what would later become known as the Australia Zoo. Initially named Beerwah Reptile and Fauna Park, it evolved over time into one of the most prominent zoos in the world. This sanctuary not only provided a safe haven for countless animals but also served as the inspiration behind Steve Irwin Day.

Steve's journey towards global recognition began at an early age. As though living out a real-life adventure story like Mowgli or Tarzan, he grew up alongside a remarkable array of creatures. By six years old, he was entrusted with a twelve-foot python as a pet—a testament to his natural affinity with animals. At just nine years old, under the watchful eye of his father, Steve wrestled his first crocodile, showcasing a fearlessness that would become one of his defining characteristics.

June 4, 1992 Steve married Terri Irwin, a woman who shared his profound love for wildlife. Their honeymoon adventures, spent capturing crocodiles on film, formed the basis for the first episode of "The Crocodile Hunter," the television series that propelled Steve Irwin into international stardom. His infectious personality and genuine passion for wildlife made him an instant hit with audiences worldwide, transforming him into a beloved pop culture icon.

Tragedy struck on September 4, 2006, during a diving expedition while filming "Ocean's Deadliest." In a shocking turn of events, Steve was fatally wounded when a stingray pierced his heart. The news sent shockwaves around the world and left millions devastated by the loss of such an incredible conservationist and advocate for animals.

To honor Steve's memory and pay tribute to his extraordinary contributions to wildlife conservation, a public memorial service was held. It garnered an unprecedented global viewership of over 300 million people—an indication of just how deeply he had touched hearts across continents.

Steve's impact extended far beyond his charismatic television persona. He was genuinely committed to making a difference in the world by fighting against illegal poaching and advocating for endangered species' protection. Through projects like Wildlife Warriors Worldwide and initiatives at Australia Zoo, he inspired countless individuals to take action towards preserving our planet's precious biodiversity.

As we celebrate Steve Irwin Day each year on November 15th, we not only commemorate the life of this remarkable man but also carry forward his mission. It is an opportunity to reflect on our own role in protecting wildlife habitats and raising awareness about environmental issues that threaten our natural world. Let us honor Steve's legacy by embracing his passion, courage, and unwavering dedication to conservation.

Steve Irwin Day stands as a testament to the enduring impact of an extraordinary individual who dedicated his life to wildlife conservation. From his childhood adventures to his rise to international fame, Steve captivated audiences with his infectious love for animals and unyielding commitment to their protection. Though his tragic passing left a void in the hearts of millions, his spirit lives on through the continued celebrations of Steve Irwin Day. So let us come together on November 15th each year, united in our reverence for this remarkable wildlife hero, as we strive to carry forward his mission of preserving and cherishing our planet's invaluable natural treasures.

In a truly awe-inspiring moment, the talented Bindi took center stage during the 81st Annual Macy's Thanksgiving Day Parade on November 22, 2007. With her infectious energy and undeniable charisma, she performed songs from her album "Trouble in the Jungle" alongside The Crocmen on a magnificent jungle animal float.

The parade was already a spectacle to behold, but Bindi's presence added an extra touch of excitement and wonder. As part of Animal Planet's "Animal Wonders" float, she showcased her passion for wildlife conservation and entertained the crowd with her captivating performance.

Sharing this incredible experience with her mother Terri,

Bindi brought joy to millions as they watched in amazement. It was a truly unforgettable moment that highlighted not only Bindi's talent but also her dedication to raising awareness about our precious animal kingdom.

Bindi's participation in the Macy's Thanksgiving Day Parade showcased her ability to captivate audiences of all ages while spreading an important message about protecting our planet and its remarkable creatures. It was a proud moment for both Bindi and Animal Planet, leaving us all in awe of their commitment to making a positive impact through their work.

The crowd was captivated as Bindi showcased her passion for wildlife conservation and her undeniable love for animals. The Animal Planet's "Animal Wonders" float came to life with vibrant colors and larger-than-life animal replicas, creating an immersive experience for all spectators.

But what made this moment even more special was the presence of Bindi's mother, Terri performed "Jump" with her daughter by her side. Together, they shared their unwavering commitment to protecting our planet's incredible biodiversity.

Bindi's performance on the jungle animal float not only entertained but also served as a reminder of the importance of environmental awareness and conservation efforts. It was a truly awe-inspiring moment that left everyone in awe of Bindi's talent and dedication to making a difference in the world.

This unforgettable performance will forever be etched in the memories of those fortunate enough to witness it firsthand. Bindi continues to be an inspiration to us all as she uses her platform to spread awareness about wildlife preservation and inspire future generations to take action.

In a remarkable turn of events, renowned psychic medium John Edward claims to have facilitated a communication between the late Steve Irwin and his wife Terri, as well as his father Bob Irwin. This extraordinary encounter took place just hours before John's performance at Australia Zoo Crocoseum January 5, 2008. As we delve into this intriguing story, we will explore the details of these alleged interactions and the profound impact they had on Terri and Bindi.

Terri, still grieving the loss of her beloved husband who tragically passed away in 2006 from a stingray's barb, sought solace in a private "reading" with John. With hopes of receiving a message from Steve's spirit, Terri met with John, who had been a close friend of her late husband. Meanwhile, Bob Irwin also engaged in his own private session with the psychic medium. Little did they know that these encounters would unveil an otherworldly connection.

Bob expressed his joy over the outcome of their meetings with John, affirming that both he and Terri had made contact with Steve's spirit. Although he refrained from disclosing specific details about the readings or the messages conveyed by John, he was certain about one thing – "There's no doubt that Steve was with us," Bob stated emphatically. He described an undeniable energy that could only be attributed to his son's presence: "It's not black and white; it's gray." The spiritual connection was real.

As John took to the stage for his public show, the audience of 4500 people anticipated a possible encounter with Steve Irwin's spirit. However, to their disappointment, John did not address any member of the Irwin family during his two-hour performance. Nevertheless, Terri took the opportunity to address the crowd and acknowledge their collective yearning to hear from the Crocodile Hunter himself. She reminded everyone that Steve's spirit was omnipresent: "If any of you are wondering why Steve didn't come through, it's because look around you, he's everywhere."

Bob expressed his belief that his son would have embraced this spiritual connection wholeheartedly while retaining his humility: "He never would have admitted it, mate." This sentiment resonated with Terri as well. Despite her deep grief, she sensed Steve's presence and had unwavering faith in his continued existence in some ethereal form: "I know he's gone, but in some way he is still here. I feel him; I sense him." The encounter with John only served to reinforce these convictions.

John Edward rose to fame through his television show Crossing Over, where he harnesses his unique abilities as a psychic medium to connect individuals with their departed loved ones. While skeptics may question the validity of such encounters and communications from beyond the grave, for those who experience them firsthand, they can be transformative and healing moments that provide solace and closure.

As we reflect on this extraordinary event involving John Edward and the Irwin family, we are left contemplating the mysteries of life and death, and the enduring connections that transcend physical boundaries. The spiritual realm continues to captivate our imagination and offers comfort for those seeking solace after losing loved ones.

Prepare to be amazed as the dynamic duo, Bindi and Terri, graced the stage once again on The Ellen DeGeneres Show for an unforgettable appearance during Season 5. The date was January 21, 2008, and they were there to captivate the audience with their incredible stories about their beloved Australia Zoo.

And what better time to showcase their Australian roots than during Aussie Week on Ellen's show? The Irwins took this opportunity to highlight the beauty and diversity of their homeland, leaving viewers yearning for a taste of Down Under.

I for one was absolutely amazed by the incredible appearance of Bindi and Terri on The Ellen DeGeneres Show when they graced the stage to talk about their remarkable Australia Zoo, where they reside. Can you believe it?

Bindi, known for her passion for wildlife conservation, shared her adventures of riding horses and ponies at the zoo. Can you imagine the thrill of galloping alongside these majestic creatures? It's a sight that surely leaves anyone in awe.

But wait, there's more! During their appearance, they also discussed some fascinating creatures like hairless rats and naked mole rats in Africa. How extraordinary! And let's not forget about chinchillas, which are unfortunately used for making coats. It's truly eye-opening to learn about these unique animals and the challenges they face.

Bindi and Terri Irwin also touched upon an important topic – the need to stop buying animal products from farmed animals and wildlife. Their commitment to conservation is truly inspiring.

I can't help but be in awe of Bindi and Terri's dedication to wildlife preservation and their efforts to spread awareness on platforms like The Ellen DeGeneres Show. They are making a significant impact in protecting our precious animal kingdom.

Let us all join them in their mission to protect these incredible creatures by stopping our consumption of animal products. Together, we can make a positive change for the future of our planet.

Bindi made a stylish appearance at the G'Day USA: Australia Week 2008 benefit for Wildlife Warriors. She ditched her usual Australia Zoo khaki uniform. Instead she opted for a flattering pastel dress and sandals. The event took place at Jazz at Lincoln Center in New York City on January 22, 2008. Bindi's attendance at this prestigious event showcased her commitment to wildlife conservation and her ability to effortlessly transition from her conservation work to the glitz and glamor of a high-profile benefit.

While at the event Bindi and her mother got friendly with Church of Scientology John Travolta with some people saying the meeting between Terri, Bindi and John led to the Church of Scientology trying to persuade Bindi into joining the controversial religion.

Bindi Irwin and John Travolta at the G'DAY USA: Australia Week gala in New York (Photo credit Laura Cavanaugh/UPI)

After meeting Church of Scientology Celebrity member John Travolta at the event Terri and Bindi continue to be friendly with him in the years to come.

The Church of Scientology, founded by L. Ron Hubbard, has gained notoriety for its association with high-profile individuals. It first opened its doors in Los Angeles and has since expanded its reach globally, establishing Celebrity Centre International in Los Angeles and several smaller celebrity centers worldwide.

Known for its unique beliefs and practices, the Church of Scientology has attracted attention from both supporters and critics alike. While some view it as a legitimate religious organization, others have raised concerns about its methods and alleged controversies.

Regardless of one's perspective, the Church of Scientology remains an intriguing subject that continues to captivate public interest.

Shortly after Bindi and Terri attended the G'Day USA event with John Travolta. Social media outlets went as far as to claim The Church of Scientology was trying to court Bindi by claiming 'She is an inspiration to people young and old – and there is no doubt Scientology would love to bring her on board.'

It's no secret Scientology leaders lean on celeb figureheads to promote the church. Celebrities like Tom Cruise, John Travolta and Kirstie Alley have long touted the religion in Hollywood.

A former member of the Church of Scientology Celebrity Centre operative Steve Mango claimed that Scientology wanted Bindi as their next celebrity recruiter and poster child. Mango was also a poster child for the church with his face put on promotional posters and brochures for the Church of

Scientology during his four years within the church from the year 2008 to 2011.

Mango claimed, "*Scientology wanted Bindi because she was a positive role model.*" With one other Scientology source adding, "You couldn't ask for a better poster child for recruitment than the beautiful daughter of a lost and beloved national figure." However Terri has claimed she would never let any of her kids anywhere near the organization, but Terri's opinion about the Church could have changed over the years.

Prepare to be amazed again by the incredible Bindi Irwin and her groundbreaking achievements on Discovery Kids' "Bindi the Jungle Girl"! This captivating documentary not only entertained audiences, but also played a pivotal role in spreading awareness about wildlife conservation.

In 2008 on May 31st the last of 26 episodes of Season 1 aired on Discovery Kids "Bindi the Jungle Girl." The documentary helped to spread the idea of wildlife conversation teaching and showing everyone in the world about the many different types of animals while explaining why they are so important to everyone and everything.

Bindi Irwin in Bindi The Jungle Girl (Photo credit: Discovery Kids)

Hold your breath, because Bindi's talent and dedication did not go unnoticed. In fact, she made history by becoming the youngest person ever to win a Daytime Emmy! Her outstanding performance in the "Children's Series" category was recognized with this prestigious award, solidifying her place as a true trailblazer in the industry.

Through "Bindi: The Jungle Girl," Bindi Irwin showcased her passion for wildlife and captured hearts around the world. Her ability to connect with both young and old audiences alike is truly awe-inspiring. Discovery Kids provided a platform for Bindi to share her knowledge, enthusiasm, and commitment to conservation, leaving an indelible mark on viewers of all ages.

Through this documentary series, Bindi not only entertained young minds but also spread awareness about wildlife conservation. She used her platform to teach children about the importance of protecting our planet's precious creatures and their habitats.

The impact of Bindi's work cannot be overstated. Her influence on younger generations has inspired countless individuals to take action and become advocates for wildlife conservation themselves. It is truly remarkable how someone so young has made such a significant impact on our world.

Bindi's journey as an advocate for wildlife conservation continues to inspire us all. Her dedication and passion serve as a shining example of what can be achieved when we combine our talents with a cause greater than ourselves.

So let's give a standing ovation to Bindi for her remarkable achievement as the youngest person ever to win a Daytime Emmy and for using her platform on "Bindi: The Jungle Girl" to promote wildlife conservation like never before. She is an inspiration to us all!

Oh my goodness, let me tell you about this incredible event that happened on October 11, 2008! Bindi, the amazing wildlife warrior, attended the 6th Annual Nickelodeon Australian Kids Choice Awards at the Hisense Arena in Melbourne. Can you imagine being at the biggest party for kids on the planet? It must have been absolutely mind-blowing!

On that special day, Bindi shared the stage with none other than John Cena and Natalie Bassingthwaighte who were hosting the show. I can only imagine how thrilled she must have been to be in such great company.

But wait, there's more! Bindi the Wildlife Warrior was not only present at this star-studded event, but she also took home two incredible awards. She won both "Biggest Greenie" and "Fave Aussie." How inspiring is that? Bindi's dedication to wildlife conservation truly shines through, and it's no wonder she was recognized for her outstanding efforts.

The Nickelodeon's Australian Kids Choice Award night was filled with excitement, laughter, and green goo galore. Bindi shone brightly as she received two well-deserved awards for her outstanding work in conservation and her exceptional role as an ambassador for wildlife. Through this celebration of Australian excellence, we are reminded of the profound impact that one person can have when they follow their passion and dedicate themselves to making a difference.

The magic of Nickelodeon's Australian Kids Choice Awards lies not only in the recognition of outstanding achievements but also in its ability to create an unforgettable experience for both attendees and viewers at home. This unique televised event brings together beloved celebrities, captivating performances, and surprises around every corner. It offers fans a chance to see their favorite stars up close while creating lifelong memories.

This event truly sounds like a dream come true for any young environmentalist or fan of Bindi. To be surrounded by so much excitement and positivity while celebrating achievements in entertainment and environmentalism must have been an experience of a lifetime.

Prepare to be amazed once again by Bindi, the incredible Wildlife Warrior, as we delve into a momentous occasion in her life. On November 13, 2009, Bindi graced the stage of the 7th Annual Australian Nickelodeon Kids Choice Awards at the prestigious Hisense Arena in Melbourne. Can you believe it? Bindi was not only a guest at this star-studded event but also emerged victorious, winning not just one, but two coveted awards!

The first accolade bestowed upon our remarkable young conservationist was the Fave Aussie award. This recognition undoubtedly reflects Bindi's immense popularity and the admiration she has garnered from fans across Australia.

Now, let's take a moment to soak in the magnitude of this extraordinary event. The 7th Annual Australian Nickelodeon Kids Choice Awards was nothing short of a spectacle – an extravaganza that brought together kids from all corners of Australia for what can only be described as the biggest kids party ever seen! Imagine being amidst such excitement and joy!

But let us not forget that this night also belonged to our incredible duo – Bindi and her brother Robert who both won the "Biggest Greenie" award. Together, they triumphed on that illustrious stage, leaving an indelible mark on Australian entertainment history.

Bindi continues to inspire us with her unwavering dedication to wildlife conservation and her infectious enthusiasm for making a positive impact on our planet. Her achievements at the 7th Annual Nickelodeon Australian Kids Choice Awards serve as a testament to her immense talent and enduring legacy.

Let us bask in awe at these remarkable accomplishments and celebrate the extraordinary journey of Bindi alongside her brother Robert – truly an unforgettable night filled with glitz, glamor, and boundless joy!

In 2010 Bindi, the fearless conservationist, embarked on an

exciting new venture. She launched her very own book series titled "Bindi Wildlife Adventures," which features a total of 20 captivating books. Each installment takes readers on a thrilling journey through the mesmerizing world of wildlife, filled with adventure, danger, and heartwarming moments.

Book 1: Trouble at the Zoo

The inaugural book in Bindi's Wildlife Adventures series is aptly titled "Trouble at the Zoo." In this gripping story, we follow Bindi as she encounters a series of mysterious incidents that disrupt the peaceful lives of animals residing at Australia Zoo. With her unwavering determination and quick thinking, Bindi embarks on an exhilarating quest to uncover the truth behind these disturbances. As readers turn each page, they are drawn into a world where bravery and compassion go hand in hand.

Book 2: Rescue!

In "Rescue!", Bindi takes us on yet another adrenaline-fueled adventure. This time, she finds herself facing a treacherous situation when an injured animal desperately needs her help. With her passion for wildlife conservation driving her every action, Bindi fearlessly dives into action to save this vulnerable creature from harm's way. Through vivid descriptions and heart-pounding moments, readers are transported to the frontlines of rescue missions alongside our courageous young protagonist.

Book 3: Bushfire!

In "Bushfire!", Bindi confronts one of nature's most devastating forces – fire. When flames engulf vast stretches of land surrounding Australia Zoo during peak fire season, Bindi must navigate through dangerous terrain to protect the animals under her care. Alongside a team of dedicated firefighters and wildlife experts, she battles against time and the destructive power of flames to ensure the safety of every creature. This thrilling installment not only sheds light on the importance of fire safety but also highlights Bindi's unwavering commitment to protecting wildlife in the face of adversity.

Book 4: Camouflage

In "Camouflage," Bindi explores the fascinating world of animal adaptations. As she embarks on a journey through lush rainforests and sprawling savannahs, Bindi encounters creatures expertly blending into their surroundings through camouflage. Through her eyes, readers discover how animals utilize their unique abilities to thrive in their respective habitats. With breathtaking illustrations and captivating anecdotes, this book opens our minds to the wonders of nature's ingenious designs.

Book 5: A Whale a Time

Prepare to be swept away by the awe-inspiring majesty of marine life in "A Whale a Time." Bindi sets sail on an oceanic adventure where she encounters magnificent whales as they migrate across vast distances. Through whimsical storytelling, readers are introduced to these gentle giants and gain insight into their behaviors, social structures, and the challenges they face in an ever-changing environment. Dive deep into this underwater voyage alongside Bindi as she unravels secrets hidden beneath the surface.

As we've explored just a handful of books from Bindi's Wildlife Adventures series, it becomes clear that each installment offers a unique blend of excitement, education, and an unwavering love for animals. Whether you're an avid reader or an enthusiast for wildlife conservation, delving into these pages will ignite your imagination and leave you yearning for more. Bindi's words transport you into a world where adventure awaits at every turn – a world where we can all become champions for wildlife.

Book 6: Roar!

In "Roar!," Bindi takes us deep into the untamed wilderness where she encounters some of Australia's most majestic predators. From lions prowling through grasslands to tigers stalking their prey in dense jungles, Bindi fearlessly explores different habitats around the world to understand these magnificent creatures better. Through her eyes, we witness breathtaking moments filled with awe as she shares stories about animal behavior, survival instincts, and the importance of protecting endangered species.

With her signature warmth and enthusiasm, Bindi brings

these animals to life on the pages of "Roar!." She details her firsthand experiences observing big cats in their natural habitats while also shedding light on the challenges they face due to habitat loss and poaching. The book serves as a reminder that every action we take can make a difference in preserving these incredible creatures for future generations.

Book 7: Croc Capers: A Bindi Irwin Adventure

In "Croc Capers: A Bindi Irwin Adventure," Bindi takes us on a thrilling escapade into the world of crocodiles. From the mighty saltwater crocodile to the elusive freshwater species, she unravels the mysteries surrounding these ancient reptiles. With her trademark bravery and infectious enthusiasm, Bindi recounts her encounters with crocs—both heart-stopping and awe-inspiring.

Through vivid storytelling and eye-opening facts, Bindi educates readers about the vital role crocodiles play in maintaining healthy ecosystems. She emphasizes the importance of coexisting with these fascinating creatures while sharing valuable insights into their behavior, feeding habits, and conservation status. "Croc Capers" is an enthralling journey that will leave you spellbound by the incredible resilience of these prehistoric predators.

Book 8: Surfing with Turtles

Dive into an underwater adventure like no other as Bindi introduces us to the captivating world of sea turtles in "Surfing with Turtles." In this book, she combines her love for marine life and passion for ocean conservation to shed light on the challenges faced by these magnificent creatures. Join Bindi as she explores coral reefs, witnesses mesmerizing nesting rituals, and learns about the threats endangering sea turtles' survival.

Through her heartfelt stories and engaging anecdotes, Bindi illustrates how our actions impact marine ecosystems and emphasizes individual responsibility in protecting these gentle giants. "Surfing with Turtles" not only immerses readers in a world teeming with beauty, but also inspires them to become advocates for marine conservation.

6

CHAPTER 6

———

In 2011 Bindi went on to release the other 11 books in her Bindi Wildlife Adventures children's Series. Here are the rest of her children's books she released.

Book 9: Lost!

In "Lost!," Bindi takes readers on an enthralling journey deep into the jungle. As she encounters various animals and navigates through treacherous terrain, Bindi learns important lessons about survival and resilience. This action-packed adventure not only keeps young readers on the edge of their seats but also imparts valuable knowledge about the delicate balance of nature.

Book 10: Monkey Mayhem

Prepare for chaos and mischief in "Monkey Mayhem"! When mischievous primates wreak havoc at Australia Zoo, it's up to Bindi and her friends to restore order. Alongside heartwarming animal encounters, this book emphasizes the importance of teamwork and problem-solving skills. Through her stories, Bindi inspires children to embrace challenges head-on while fostering a deep love for wildlife.

Book 11: A Giant Rescue

In "A Giant Rescue," Bindi embarks on a mission to save an endangered species from harm's way. With determination and bravery, she faces formidable obstacles to protect these majestic creatures. This book highlights the significance of conservation efforts and instills in young minds a profound sense of responsibility towards our planet's biodiversity.

Book 12: Mission Climate Change

As climate change continues to pose threats to ecosystems worldwide, Bindi tackles this pressing issue in "Mission Climate Change." Through her adventures, she educates readers about the importance of sustainable practices and the impact of human actions on the environment. This book serves as a call to action, urging young readers to become stewards of the Earth and make a positive difference for future generations.

Book 13: Snow Monkey Mischief

In "Snow Monkey Mischief," Bindi takes readers on an

enchanting journey through wintry landscapes. Amidst playful snow monkeys and breathtaking scenery, Bindi explores the wonders of cold climates. This book not only highlights the beauty of nature but also encourages children to embrace curiosity and explore new environments with an open mind.

Book 15: Bears Beware!

"Bears Beware!" delves into the realm of these magnificent creatures, shedding light on their habitats and behaviors. Bindi's encounters with bears emphasize the importance of respect and understanding when coexisting with wildlife. Through this book, young readers develop empathy towards animals while learning about conservation efforts aimed at protecting bear species worldwide.

A Wildlife Safari: Book 16 – Rhino Safari

In "Rhino Safari," Bindi takes us on an exhilarating journey through the African savannah. Joined by her friends and family, she encounters endangered rhinos up close while highlighting the importance of conservation efforts to protect these majestic creatures. Through vivid descriptions and captivating storytelling, Bindi paints a picture that transports readers to the heart of Africa's wilderness.

Scaling New Heights: Book 17 – Silverback Mountain

The adventure continues in "Silverback Mountain" as Bindi embarks on an expedition to study gorillas in their natural habitat. As she treks through dense forests and encounters these awe-inspiring primates, readers are introduced to the world of gorilla conservation. With each turn of the page, Bindi showcases her passion for wildlife preservation while educating young minds about these incredible animals.

Unveiling Island Secrets: Book 18 – Island Ambush

In "Island Ambush," Bindi sets sail on an exciting escapade to an exotic island teeming with unique wildlife. As she navigates through lush rainforests and encounters rare species found nowhere else on earth, readers are immersed in a world brimming with biodiversity. Bindi's vivid descriptions and attention to detail make this adventure come alive, captivating young readers and sparking curiosity about the wonders of our planet.

A Battle for Survival: Book 19 – Trapped!

"Trapped!" introduces readers to a thrilling tale of danger and resilience. Bindi finds herself caught in an unexpected situation while exploring a treacherous wilderness. As she faces numerous challenges and tests her survival skills, young readers are taken on an emotional rollercoaster, learning valuable lessons about resilience, determination, and the importance of teamwork.

Pandemonium in Paradise: Book 20 – Panda-Monium

The final installment in the "Bindi Wildlife Adventures" series, "Panda-Monium," takes us on a journey to the enchanting bamboo forests of China. Bindi's encounter with adorable giant pandas sheds light on their conservation status and the efforts being made to protect these gentle giants. Through heartwarming storytelling and beautiful illustrations, Bindi leaves readers with a lasting appreciation for these iconic creatures.

Bindi's "Bindi Wildlife Adventures" book series is more than just an exciting collection of tales; it serves as a powerful call to action for readers of all ages. Through her remarkable experiences and deep understanding of wildlife conservation, Bindi implores us to embrace our role as custodians of the Earth and protect the incredible biodiversity that surrounds us. With each page turned, we embark on a journey filled with wonder, knowledge, and a renewed commitment to preserving our natural world.

Prepare to be amazed once again by Bindi the incredible Wildlife Warrior, as we delve into a momentous occasion in her life. On November 13, 2009, Bindi graced the stage of the 7th Annual Australian Nickelodeon Kids Choice Awards at the prestigious Hisense Arena in Melbourne. Can you believe it? Bindi was not only a guest at this star-studded event but also emerged victorious, winning not just one, but two coveted awards!

The first accolade bestowed upon our remarkable young conservationist won the "Fave Aussie" award. This recognition undoubtedly reflects Bindi's immense popularity and the admiration she has garnered from fans across Australia. But that's not all! Bindi's dedication to environmental causes and her unwavering passion for protecting our planet earned her another prestigious title – the Biggest Greenie award.

Now, let's take a moment to soak in the magnitude of this extraordinary event. The 7th Annual Australian Nickelodeon Kids Choice Awards was nothing short of a spectacle – an extravaganza that brought together kids from all corners of Australia for what can only be described as the biggest kids party ever seen! Imagine being amidst such excitement and joy!

But let us not forget that this night belonged to our incredible duo – Bindi and her brother Robert Irwin won "Biggest Greenie". Together, they triumphed on that illustrious stage, leaving an indelible mark on Australian entertainment history.

Bindi Irwin continues to inspire us with her unwavering dedication to wildlife conservation and her infectious enthusiasm for making a positive impact on our planet. Her achievements at the 7th Annual Nickelodeon Australian Kids

Choice Awards serve as a testament to her immense talent and enduring legacy.

Let us bask in awe at these remarkable accomplishments and celebrate the extraordinary journey of Bindi Irwin alongside her brother Robert – truly an unforgettable night filled with glitz, glamor, and boundless joy!

When it comes to heartwarming family films, few can rival the timeless charm of the Free Willy franchise. The fourth installment, "Free Willy: Escape from Pirate's Cove," aired March 23, 2010. It introduces us to a new generation of characters and captivating performances – none more delightful than Bindi as the film's star.

Bindi Irwin in the film Free Willy: Escape from Pirate's Cove (Photo credit Warner Bros, warner Bros. Home Entertainment, Warner Premiere)

"Escape from Pirate's Cove" follows the journey of Kira (played by Bindi Irwin), a young girl faced with unexpected challenges. After her father sustains an injury in a farming accident, Kira finds herself sent to stay with her eccentric grandfather, Gus (portrayed by Beau Bridges). The seaside amusement park he owns becomes their unlikely meeting place. Both grappling with personal loss and seeking solace in their shared love for someone dear to them, Kira and Gus embark on a journey that will change their lives forever.

Nestled within the stunning landscapes of South Africa, "Escape from Pirate's Cove" captures the beauty of this diverse country. From its rugged coastline to its vibrant wildlife reserves, South Africa provides an awe-inspiring backdrop for this heartwarming tale. As Kira finds herself amidst her grandfather's seaside amusement park, viewers are treated to glimpses of South Africa's rich culture and natural wonders.

In her portrayal of Kira, Bindi Irwin shines brightly as a rising star in the world of acting. Following in the footsteps of her legendary father Steve Irwin – known as the Crocodile Hunter – Bindi brings her own unique charm and talent to the screen. Despite her young age at the time of filming, Bindi's performance showcases a depth and maturity beyond her years. She effortlessly captures Kira's emotional journey, allowing us to connect with and root for her character throughout the film.

"Escape from Pirate's Cove" marks a departure from the previous Free Willy films, serving as both a soft reboot and a standalone story within the franchise. While the iconic orca whale named Willy is absent from this installment, the film offers its own brand of magic, centered around an adorable baby whale who finds himself trapped in Gus' amusement park lagoon. As Kira develops a bond with this majestic creature, she and Gus must navigate challenges and ultimately work together to save him from those who would exploit him for profit.

Though "Escape from Pirate's Cove" may feature some CGI substitutes for real whales, it makes up for it with its genuine emotional moments. The filmmakers masterfully infuse the story with heartfelt scenes that tug at our heartstrings – most notably when Gus reflects on his shortcomings as a father and confronts his past mistakes. Beau Bridges delivers a truly heartbreaking performance as he contemplates his life's regrets, reminding us that it is never too late for redemption.

As we delve into "Free Willy: Escape from Pirate's Cove," we are transported to an enchanting world filled with family bonds, stunning landscapes, and captivating performances – particularly Bindi's delightful portrayal of Kira. This film proves that even without the original Willy in tow, there is still plenty of magic to be found in this beloved franchise. So gather your loved ones and prepare to embark on an unforgettable adventure filled with laughter, tears, and the profound joy that comes from experiencing cinema at its finest.

Back on December 14, 2010, the world eagerly tuned in to witness an extraordinary meeting between iconic figures: Bindi and Oprah Winfrey. This momentous occasion took place on the set of "The Oprah Winfrey Show" at the Sydney Opera House, where Oprah herself had descended along with 302 lucky superfans from across North America and Jamaica. They were all there to be a part of history as Oprah filmed four shows for her 25th and final season.

On that memorable day, Oprah welcomed Terri, Bindi, and Robert onto her stage. The audience erupted in cheers as these beloved members of the renowned Crocodile Hunter family made their entrance. The excitement was palpable, as everyone knew they were about to witness something truly special.

Terri, Bindi and Robert Irwin with Oprah Winfrey at the Sydney Opera House (Photo credit: The Oprah Winfrey Show)

Known for her unwavering passion for wildlife conservation and her captivating presence in front of the camera, Bindi had already amassed a substantial following by the time she appeared on "The Oprah Winfrey Show." Her infectious enthusiasm and dedication to preserving wildlife habitats had earned her a place among Australia's most beloved personalities.

During their conversation on stage, Bindi shared stories about growing up at Australia Zoo and carrying forward her father's mission. She spoke passionately about the importance of protecting our planet's biodiversity and inspiring others to take action. With each word she uttered, it became evident that Bindi possessed not only her father's love for animals but also his ability to captivate audiences with genuine warmth.

Oprah recognized the profound impact Bindi was making at such a young age and expressed her admiration for the young wildlife warrior. Together, they discussed the significance of educating future generations about the environment and fostering a deep connection with nature. Bindi's unwavering dedication to conservation resonated with Oprah, who herself had used her platform to advocate for numerous causes over the years.

By appearing on "The Oprah Winfrey Show," Bindi Irwin was given an unprecedented opportunity to reach millions of viewers worldwide. Her presence on that stage not only amplified her voice but also shed light on the urgent need for environmental stewardship. Bindi's infectious passion ignited a fire within those who watched, inspiring countless individuals to take action and make a positive difference in their own lives.

The impact of Bindi's appearance on "The Oprah Winfrey Show" continues to reverberate today. Her message of conservation and love for wildlife remains as relevant as ever, inspiring a new generation to stand up and protect our planet's precious ecosystems. Through her work, Bindi has become an influential role model, proving that age is no barrier when it comes to making a lasting impact.

As we look back on that fateful day in 2010 when Bindi Irwin graced the stage of "The Oprah Winfrey Show," it is clear that this meeting marked an indelible moment in both television history and the world of wildlife conservation. The synergy between two influential figures allowed their shared passion for creating positive change to shine through.

In their exchange of ideas and stories, Bindi and Oprah reminded us all of our responsibility as stewards of this planet. They showed us that by embracing our individual voices and taking action, we have the power to make a profound difference in the world around us.

Bindi, the 12-year-old author and wildlife conservationist, made a captivating return to the iconic Oprah Winfrey Show in Australia: Ultimate Wildest Dreams on January 20, 2011. Joined by her resilient family, Bindi shared her remarkable journey of growing up in the footsteps of her late father. Bindi's appearance on the Oprah Winfrey Show was a heartwarming interview that touched millions of viewers.

Terri, Bindi and Robert Irwin with Oprah Winfrey at the Sydney Opera House in Australia: Ultimate Wildest Dreams (Photo credit: The Oprah Winfrey Show)

In a poignant moment during their appearance on the show, Terri opened up about her experience navigating life after losing her beloved husband. She shared on the show empowering words on moving forward after the loss of her husband, Steve. With grace and resilience, Terri shared how she and her two extraordinary children have found strength despite their immense loss.

Terri's words echoed with hope and determination as she spoke about carrying on Steve's legacy through their shared passion for wildlife conservation. She emphasized that while grief is an ongoing process, it should not define one's future. Instead, Terri encouraged viewers to find solace in cherishing cherished memories while embracing new beginnings.

Bindi and Robert stood beside their mother throughout the interview, embodying their father's spirit and enthusiasm for preserving nature. Their presence showcased not only their own resilience but also served as a reminder of Steve's enduring impact on his family.

During the show, viewers were treated to an exclusive video tour of Australia Zoo led by none other than Bindi Irwin herself. As the camera panned across the sprawling grounds of the zoo located in Brisbane, Bindi shared fascinating insights and introduced various animals that call Australia Zoo their home.

From cuddly koalas to slithering snakes, Bindi walked us through the diverse range of wildlife found within the zoo's walls. Her infectious passion for animal conservation shone through as she shared stories about each creature's unique characteristics and the importance of protecting their natural habitats.

As we journeyed alongside Bindi, it became clear why Australia Zoo is not just a place but a sanctuary—a sacred space where Steve's legacy lives on and where wildlife thrives under the watchful eye of his adoring family. The video tour left viewers inspired to learn more about these incredible animals and motivated to play their part in preserving our planet's biodiversity.

In addition to her awe-inspiring television appearances, Bindi Irwin has also made a name for herself as an accomplished author. Her debut book, Trouble at the Zoo, marks the beginning of her Wildlife Adventures series—an enchanting collection that combines captivating storytelling with important lessons about conservation.

Through her books, Bindi takes readers on thrilling adventures set within the world-renowned Australia Zoo. Each story intertwines engaging narratives with valuable insights into environmental issues and wildlife protection. Young readers are not only entertained by these tales but also educated about their role in safeguarding our planet's natural wonders.

Trouble at the Zoo is just the first chapter in what promises to be an extraordinary literary journey led by Bindi Irwin. With her boundless enthusiasm and unwavering dedication to wildlife preservation, Bindi continues to inspire young minds across the globe, encouraging them to become stewards of our fragile ecosystems.

Bindi's appearance on the Oprah Winfrey Show was a triumphant testament to her unwavering spirit, innate wisdom, and commitment to making a difference in the world. Her family's journey of resilience touched the hearts of millions, reminding us all of the power of love, determination, and embracing life's challenges head-on.

As we reflect on Bindi's inspiring return to the Oprah Winfrey Show, we are compelled to carry forward her message—a message that encourages us to channel our passion into positive action. Whether it be through supporting wildlife conservation efforts, cherishing cherished memories, or finding strength amidst adversity—Bindi has shown us that age is no barrier when it comes to creating lasting change.

Bindi has continued her father's legacy by becoming an influential figure in wildlife conservation. In 2012, Bindi took on the role of Earth Hour Ambassador on March 30, 2012 and she launched her own television series called "Bindi's Bootcamp" on July 7, 2012. This captivating show, filmed at Australia Zoo aired on ABC3. It aimed to educate and test contestants' knowledge about wildlife through thrilling adventure challenges. Bindi's television series inspired a generation to protect our planet's precious ecosystems.

In July 2012, Bindi embarked on a new endeavor that would combine education and adventure in an unprecedented way.

"Bindi's Bootcamp" was not just any ordinary TV show; it was an immersive experience that transported viewers into the heart of Australia Zoo.

Produced by Sydney-based Sticky Pictures under commission from ABC3, this groundbreaking series aimed to inspire young minds to become passionate advocates for wildlife conservation. Contestants faced a series of adrenaline-pumping challenges designed to test their knowledge and understanding of the animal kingdom. From obstacle courses to wildlife encounters, each episode offered thrilling adventures while imparting valuable lessons about nature, biodiversity, and environmental stewardship.

"Bindi's Bootcamp" had an immediate impact on its viewers, captivating both children and adults alike. By showcasing the wonders of Australia Zoo and the importance of wildlife preservation, Bindi Irwin successfully instilled a sense of responsibility towards our natural world.

The show not only entertained but also educated its audience, fostering a deeper appreciation for the incredible diversity of animals on our planet. Through exciting challenges and interactive learning experiences, Bindi ignited a passion for conservation in the hearts of many.

Bindi's commitment to wildlife conservation did not end with "Bindi's Bootcamp". She has continued her efforts through various initiatives, including her active involvement in Australia Zoo and ongoing environmental advocacy work.

Today, Bindi remains an influential figure in inspiring people worldwide to protect our planet. Her unwavering dedication serves as a reminder that we all play a vital role in preserving Earth's delicate ecosystems. Whether it is through small everyday actions or larger-scale initiatives, we can make a difference—just like Bindi.

As we reflect on the impact of "Bindi's Bootcamp" in 2012 and beyond, let us be inspired by Bindi's unwavering commitment to wildlife conservation. Each one of us has the power to contribute positively to our environment and protect the countless species that call this planet home.

So why not embrace your own inner adventurer? Take part in local conservation projects or explore nature reserves near you. Educate yourself about different species and their habitats. Together, we can follow in Bindi's footsteps and create a future where wildlife thrives and our planet flourishes.

In 2012, she released a captivating book series called "Bindi Behind the Scenes," offering readers a fascinating glimpse into her life and adventures. Now lets explore each book in the series, diving into the thrilling stories and valuable lessons they hold. Get ready to embark on a literary journey alongside Bindi herself!

Book 1: "The Wildlife Games"

In the first installment of the "Bindi Behind the Scenes" series, titled "The Wildlife Games," Bindi takes readers on an exciting adventure filled with wildlife encounters and unforgettable moments. Join her as she navigates through challenges, both on and off-screen, to protect and conserve nature's precious creatures. Through heartwarming stories and captivating narrative, Bindi shares valuable insights about wildlife conservation while showcasing her deep connection with animals.

Book 2: "An Island Escape"

In "An Island Escape," book two of the series, Bindi finds herself in an entirely new environment—on a remote island brimming with unique flora and fauna. Readers are transported to this enchanting paradise as they join Bindi on an unforgettable journey of discovery. From encountering rare species to uncovering hidden secrets of the island's ecosystem, this book is a testament to Bindi's commitment to educating others about our planet's biodiversity.

Book 3: "A Guest Appearance"

In book three of the series, "A Guest Appearance," Bindi invites readers behind-the-scenes of her life as she embarks on exciting collaborations with fellow wildlife enthusiasts. From joining forces with renowned conservationists to working alongside animal experts, Bindi shares her experiences of making guest appearances in different wildlife-related projects. This book not only offers a unique perspective on the world of wildlife but also emphasizes the significance of collaboration and teamwork in achieving common goals.

Book 4: "Dive in Deeper"

"Dive in Deeper," book four of the series, takes readers on an immersive underwater adventure alongside Bindi as she explores the mesmerizing realm beneath the waves. From vibrant coral reefs teeming with life to encounters with magnificent marine creatures, this book delves into the wonders of the ocean. Through her storytelling prowess, Bindi encourages readers to appreciate and protect our planet's precious marine ecosystems.

Book 5: "Bouncing off the Menu"

In "Bouncing off the Menu," Bindi Irwin combines her passion for wildlife conservation with her love for healthy living and sustainable choices. Join her as she explores mindful eating habits and shares delicious recipes inspired by nature's bounty. With a focus on promoting sustainable practices and supporting local communities, this book serves as a valuable guide for individuals seeking to make a positive impact through their dietary choices.

Book 6: "A Ghostly Take"

The final installment of the "Bindi Behind the Scenes" series, titled "A Ghostly Take," ventures into an unconventional territory—ghost stories! In this thrilling book, Bindi intertwines spine-tingling tales with important lessons about environmental preservation. By highlighting how human actions can impact both the living and non-living inhabitants of our planet, she reminds readers of their responsibility to protect and cherish nature.

Bindi Irwin's book series, "Bindi Behind the Scenes," offers readers a captivating blend of adventure, education, and inspiration. Through each installment, Bindi shares her deep love for wildlife while imparting valuable lessons about conservation and sustainability. Whether you're a dedicated fan of Bindi Irwin or an avid reader seeking captivating stories, these books are sure to engage and enlighten.

On October 6, 2012, a remarkable event took place that thrilled nature enthusiasts and fans of the late Steve Irwin. Bindi was awarded the lead role in the television series "Steve Irwin's Wildlife Warriors." This significant development not only marked a milestone in Bindi's career but also symbolized her commitment to carrying on her father's legacy.

Bindi was destined to follow in her father's footsteps from an early age. Growing up at Australia Zoo, surrounded by animals and immersed in wildlife conservation efforts, she developed a deep love and understanding for the natural world. Steve's passion for preserving wildlife was instilled in his daughter from the start.

As Bindi blossomed into an exceptional young woman, she began showcasing her talent and dedication to environmental causes through various mediums. From captivating appearances on television shows to writing books that inspire young readers to care for our planet, Bindi proved herself as a force to be reckoned with in the realm of conservation.

The announcement of Bindi Irwin landing the lead role in "Steve Irwin's Wildlife Warriors" created ripples of excitement among nature enthusiasts worldwide. The television series serves as both a tribute to Steve Irwin's incredible work and a platform for continuing his mission of wildlife preservation.

Episode Highlights:

1. Exploring Untouched Habitats: Each episode takes viewers on an exhilarating journey through some of Earth's most breathtaking and unexplored habitats. From the lush rainforests of the Amazon to the vast savannahs of Africa, Bindi and her team venture into these ecosystems to document unique species and

raise awareness about their conservation needs.

2. Close Encounters with Wildlife: The series offers an intimate look at wildlife encounters, allowing viewers to witness Bindi's interactions with extraordinary animals up close. Whether she is handling a slithering python or observing majestic big cats in their natural habitat, Bindi's genuine love for creatures of all kinds shines through.

3. Educational Insights: "Steve Irwin's Wildlife Warriors" goes beyond entertainment; it serves as an educational tool, providing valuable insights into environmental issues and suggesting ways individuals can make a positive impact. Each episode includes segments that highlight practical steps viewers can take to contribute to wildlife conservation efforts in their own lives.

4. Guest Appearances by Prominent Conservationists: In addition to her own adventures, Bindi invites renowned conservationists as guest stars on the show. These experts share their knowledge and experiences, inspiring viewers with their dedication to protecting our planet.

5. Empowering Young Audiences: One of the show's primary objectives is to empower young audiences to become wildlife warriors themselves. Through engaging storytelling and relatable experiences, Bindi encourages children and teenagers to embrace

their role as stewards of the environment.

Bindi's involvement in "Steve Irwin's Wildlife Warriors" not only honors her father but also amplifies his message of environmental stewardship. Through her talent, charisma, and unwavering dedication, she captivates audiences of all ages while imparting essential knowledge about wildlife preservation.

By continuing her father's work through this television series, Bindi inspires millions around the world to appreciate nature's wonders and recognize the urgent need for conservation efforts. Her infectious enthusiasm and genuine love for animals make her a powerful advocate for wildlife, ensuring that Steve's legacy lives on through the next generation of conservationists.

Bindi's lead role in "Steve Irwin's Wildlife Warriors" is a testament to her unwavering commitment to wildlife conservation. Through this television series, she educates, entertains, and empowers audiences, carrying forward the mission of her late father. Bindi's passion for wildlife preservation serves as an inspiration to us all, reminding us that we each have the power to make a positive impact on our planet and its magnificent creatures.

7

CHAPTER 7

With its captivating blend of supernatural elements and teenage drama, "My Babysitter's a Vampire" has been a favorite among fans for years since it was released on August 13, 2012. In the episode "Mirror/rorriM," talented Bindi took center stage as she portrayed Sunday Clovers, the star of the school play, "The Rainbow Factory." As the story unfolds, unexpected events cast a dark shadow over the production, leaving our beloved characters to face mysterious ghosts and unforeseen challenges.

In a twist of fate, when Bindi's character, Sunday Clovers, is mysteriously harmed during what seems like an innocent prank, Erica steps up to take on the starring role. Little do they know that this seemingly innocuous turn of events will lead them down a path filled with danger and suspense. As Erica delves deeper into her newfound role, an unexpected presence lurking within a mirror backstage begins to exert control over her every action.

As Ethan, Benny, and Sarah strive to uncover the truth behind the ghostly interference with their play, they find themselves embroiled in a race against time. The trio must decipher why this restless spirit seeks to sabotage their production before someone falls victim to its malevolent intentions. While Rory amuses himself by playing pranks on unsuspecting individuals as his alter ego "Pranksy," his comedic subplot adds an extra layer of entertainment to the episode.

Rory's mischievous endeavors as "Pranksy" offer lighthearted moments amidst the mounting tension surrounding their haunted theater. Throughout the episode, Rory struggles with anonymity until he finally reveals his secret identity in a daring act that lands him in three weeks of detention. Despite the consequences, Rory finds solace in the fact that he has finally made his mark on Whitechapel High.

While "Mirror/rorriM" delivers a thrilling storyline, some viewers may find themselves yearning for more. The episode raises intriguing questions about the origins of the ghost trapped within the mirror and leaves us craving further details.

Additionally, we glimpse Benny's magical prowess as he employs a spell and wand to rescue Ethan from his mirror-bound predicament. Exploring these elements in greater depth or delving into the events of twenty-five years ago would have added an extra layer of intrigue to this already compelling episode.

A standout aspect of "Mirror/rorriM" is Bindi Irwin's exceptional portrayal of Sunday Clovers. With her infectious energy and undeniable talent, she brings Sunday to life with remarkable authenticity. As fans reminisce about her late father's iconic show, "The Crocodile Hunter," Rory even references it in an earlier episode, reminding us of the deep connection between generations of wildlife enthusiasts.

"My Babysitter's a Vampire: Mirror/rorriM" offers an engaging and enthralling viewing experience. Bindi Irwin's magnetic performance shines amidst a backdrop of supernatural twists and turns. While some lingering questions remain unanswered, this episode captivates audiences with its blend of mystery, humor, and teenage camaraderie that has made the show a beloved favorite among fans for years.

January 24, 2013 Bindi courted controversy when she criticized the department of US Secretary of State, Hillary

Clinton, after an essay she wrote on conservation for Hillary's e-journal was heavily edited – at Bindi's request, the article was withdrawn.

The world of conservation and wildlife was rocked by the controversial incident involving a clash between Bindi and Hillary Clinton, the former US Secretary of State. In what seemed like a battle of ideologies, Bindi found herself at odds with Clinton after an essay she wrote for the Secretary's e-journal was heavily edited. The fallout from this clash raises important questions about the issue of population growth and its impact on our fragile planet.

Bindi, known for her unwavering dedication to wildlife conservation, was asked by Hillary Clinton's department to write an essay explaining why she had chosen to devote her life's work to preserving our natural world. The piece was intended for publication in an issue titled "Go Wild: Coming Together for Conservation" as part of Secretary Clinton's endangered species initiative. However, when Bindi received the final version of her essay for approval, she found it had been drastically edited.

In her essay, Bindi used a simple yet thought-provoking analogy to express her concerns about overpopulation. She compared it to throwing a party and having more guests show up than expected. She painted a vivid picture of inviting 15 close friends to her party – renting a room and preparing enough food and party favors for everyone. But when 70 people arrived at her door instead of 15, she faced a dilemma.

Bindi questioned how our fragile planet can sustain such massive population growth. With limited resources and space, dividing everything equally among the unexpected guests would leave everyone unsatisfied. This analogy encapsulates the challenges we face as our global population continues to expand beyond our planet's capacity to support it.

When Bindi received the edited version of her essay, she found that most of her original content had been removed. This drastic editing raised concerns about whether Bindi's perspective on population growth was deemed too controversial for publication. The incident ignited a heated debate about the freedom to express dissenting opinions, even when it involved high-profile figures.

The clash between Bindi Irwin and Hillary Clinton highlights the complexities surrounding discussions on population growth and its impact on our environment. It raises important questions that demand thoughtful consideration and open dialogue.

Population growth is an issue that affects every aspect of our lives – from resource distribution to environmental sustainability. It influences food security, access to healthcare, urbanization, and many other critical factors. Ignoring or silencing discussions around this topic hinders progress towards finding sustainable solutions for our planet's future.

By engaging in conversations about population growth, we can explore innovative ideas and initiatives to address its challenges. It allows us to consider alternative approaches such as education, family planning, and sustainable development practices to ensure a better future for all.

The clash between Bindi Irwin and Hillary Clinton serves as a reminder that no issue should be off-limits when it comes to respectful discourse. While conflicts may arise due to differing perspectives, it is essential to foster dialogue rather than suppress it. By encouraging open discussions about population growth and its implications, we can collectively work towards finding solutions that balance the needs of both people and our planet.

The clash between Bindi Irwin and Hillary Clinton over an edited essay also sheds light on the importance of addressing population growth openly. Through respectful dialogue and exploration of different viewpoints, we can strive for a more sustainable future that considers the well-being of both humanity and our natural world. Let us embrace these opportunities for discussion as we navigate the complex challenges facing our planet today.

In 2013, a heartwarming and unexpected event took place on the popular Australian TV series, Big Brother. Bindi made a brief appearance to surprise one of the housemates, Tim. This special moment left an indelible mark on both the contestants and viewers alike.

During the 2013 season of Big Brother Australia, contestant Tim Dormer developed quite a fondness for Bindi. He frequently mentioned her throughout his time in the house and expressed his admiration for her work as a Wildlife Warrior. Little did he know that his kind words were about to be reciprocated in a remarkable way.

In an emotional twist orchestrated by the show's producers, Bindi surprised Tim during a live episode. As he sat in the Big Brother house, unaware of what was about to unfold, Bindi appeared on the screen and addressed him directly. With her signature smile, she thanked Tim for his support and commended him for being an incredible Wildlife Warrior himself. The sheer surprise and joy on Tim's face were palpable, as he beamed with delight at this unexpected encounter.

While this moment may have seemed like just another memorable reality TV scene, its significance extends far beyond the realm of entertainment. Bindi's appearance on Big Brother served as a poignant reminder of her father's legacy and the impact he made worldwide. It showcased Bindi's own dedication to conservation and her ability to inspire others through her work.

Moreover, this heartfelt exchange highlighted the power of television in bringing people together and fostering connections. In that fleeting moment on live television, Bindi not only touched Tim's heart but also left an impression on countless viewers watching from their homes. It served as a testament to the enduring influence of Steve Irwin's message of wildlife conservation and the continued efforts carried out by his family.

One of the most significant outcomes of Bindi's surprise appearance is the inspiration it sparked in a new generation of Wildlife Warriors. By seeing someone like Bindi, who has dedicated her life to protecting animals and their habitats, young adults were reminded that they too can make a difference.

Bindi's appearance on Big Brother encouraged viewers to reflect on their own passions and consider how they could contribute positively to society. Her infectious enthusiasm ignited a flame within many hearts, motivating them to take action in protecting our planet and its precious wildlife.

It showcased her unwavering commitment to wildlife conservation, while also reminding us of the enduring legacy left by her father, Steve Irwin. This heartwarming moment not only entertained audiences but also inspired a new generation to become Wildlife Warriors themselves. Through television, Bindi continues to touch lives and spread her message of love and protection for our natural world.

If you are a fan of heartwarming family films that transport you to captivating landscapes while delivering a powerful message, then Return to Nim's Island is a movie you won't want to miss. Released on March 15, 2013, this Australian adventure-fantasy film directed by Brendan Maher brings together an incredible cast, including the talented Bindi Irwin.

At the core of Return to Nim's Island lies an important message about conservation and protecting our natural environment. The film follows the story of a scientist named Jack (played by Matthew Lillard) and his courageous daughter Nim (portrayed by Bindi Irwin). Together, they embark on an extraordinary journey to safeguard their beloved island from ruthless developers and poachers who threaten its pristine beauty.

Bindi Irwin and Toby Wallace in the film Return to Nim's Island (Photo credit: Walden Media/Arc Entertainment, Hallmark Channel)

As the plot unfolds, viewers are drawn into an adventure filled with suspense, daring escapes, and heartwarming moments. With their unwavering determination and love for their home, Jack and Nim become unlikely heroes fighting against all odds to preserve what they hold dear. It is through their bravery that they inspire others to recognize the importance of environmental conservation.

One of the highlights of Return to Nim's Island is undoubtedly the exceptional casting choice of Bindi Irwin as Nim. As the daughter of renowned wildlife expert Steve Irwin, Bindi brings not only her acting skills but also her genuine passion for wildlife conservation to her role.

Bindi's natural charisma and infectious enthusiasm shine

through in every scene, captivating audiences of all ages. Her portrayal of Nim is both endearing and empowering, showcasing a young girl who is intelligent, resourceful, and deeply connected to nature. Bindi's performance serves as a reminder of the impact passionate individuals can have when they stand up for what they believe in.

Beyond its engaging storyline and talented cast, Return to Nim's Island immerses viewers in the breathtaking beauty of Queensland's rainforests and beaches. The film makes exceptional use of its stunning setting to create a visually captivating experience that transports audiences to another world.

As you watch the movie unfold, you will find yourself mesmerized by the lush greenery of the rainforest, feeling the warmth of the sun on your skin as it filters through the canopy above. The pristine beaches with their crystal-clear waters invite you to dip your toes into their gentle waves. Through skillful cinematography and meticulous attention to detail, Return to Nim's Island showcases the splendor of nature at its finest.

What sets Return to Nim's Island apart from other family films is its ability to resonate with viewers of all ages. While children will be captivated by the thrilling adventure and delightful characters, adults will appreciate the underlying messages about environmental stewardship and the power we hold to make a difference.

The film reminds us that each one of us has a role to play in protecting our environment and preserving it for future generations. It encourages us to embrace our connection with nature and take action against those who seek to exploit it for personal gain.

Return to Nim's Island is an enchanting film that combines captivating storytelling, remarkable performances, stunning visuals, and important messages about conservation. Bindi's star presence brings an extra layer of authenticity and passion to this sun-drenched family adventure.

On April 18, 2013, something truly remarkable happened at the iconic Gardens by the Bay in Singapore. Discovery Asia had the honor of hosting Bindi and her family as they continued Steve's mission of wildlife conservation. This extraordinary event not only celebrated Bindi's dedication to carrying on her father's legacy but also highlighted the importance of preserving our natural world.

The event hosted by Discovery Asia at Gardens by the Bay

served as a tribute to Steve's incredible legacy while showcasing Bindi's unwavering commitment to animal advocacy.

Nestled amidst Singapore's urban landscape, Gardens by the Bay stands as a magnificent testament to nature's resilience. Spanning over 250 acres, this futuristic garden is a harmonious blend of technology and horticulture. Its mesmerizing Supertrees, lush flower domes, and tranquil lakes provide an enchanting backdrop for any occasion.

During this special event, Bindi Irwin and her family immersed themselves in the captivating beauty of Gardens by the Bay. Surrounded by serene greenery and breathtaking floral displays, they experienced firsthand how nature can heal and inspire.

Bindi embarked on an Asian tour that took her across Singapore, Hong Kong, Manila, and Kuala Lumpur. This tour served as a platform for her to raise awareness about the Steve Irwin Wildlife Warriors and the urgent need for wildlife conservation in the region.

In each city, Bindi engaged with local communities, sharing her father's message of environmental stewardship and inspiring individuals to take action. By collaborating with Discovery Asia, Bindi was able to reach a broader audience and ignite a passion for wildlife conservation among people from diverse backgrounds.

As part of the event at Gardens by the Bay, Discovery Asia organized a special ceremony to celebrate Bindi Irwin's extraordinary achievements. A tree was planted in her honor, symbolizing growth, resilience, and the enduring legacy she carries forward.

This act of planting trees not only pays tribute to Bindi but also serves as a call to action for all who witness it. It reminds us that we each have a role to play in creating a sustainable future for generations to come.

The event hosted by Discovery Asia at Gardens by the Bay was more than just an occasion; it was a testament to the power of one family's unwavering commitment to wildlife conservation. Through Bindi Irwin's tireless efforts, Steve's mission lives on, inspiring millions around the world.

As adults passionate about our planet's well-being, let us embrace Bindi's message and take action to protect the precious biodiversity that surrounds us. Together, we can create a world where future generations can marvel at the wonders of nature, just as Steve and Bindi have shown us.

Bindi's unwavering dedication and infectious charisma have

not gone unnoticed. She received a well-deserved nomination for the "Most Popular Female Television Presenter" at the prestigious TV Week Logie Awards. This recognition further solidifies her impact as an influential figure in the realm of wildlife advocacy and television.

Through her captivating television appearances, Bindi has inspired countless individuals to develop a deeper connection with nature and become active participants in preserving our planet's biodiversity.

In the world of television, there are rare moments when a rising star shines so brightly that their talent and charisma captivate audiences across the globe. Such is the case with Bindi, who has recently received a prestigious nomination for the "Most Popular Female Television Presenter" at the 2013 TV Week Logie Awards. This recognition not only celebrates her immense talent but also highlights her dedication to inspiring and educating viewers through her captivating presence on screen.

Bindi has been making waves in the entertainment industry from a young age. Growing up amidst wildlife and nature, she inherited her father's passion for animals and embarked on a journey to continue his legacy. Bindi's infectious enthusiasm and natural ability to connect with both people and wildlife have solidified her place as an influential figure in television.

The TV Week Logie Awards are one of Australia's most esteemed television accolades, celebrating excellence in local television programming. Each year, these awards recognize outstanding performances and contributions made by actors, presenters, writers, directors, and other industry professionals who have left an indelible mark on Australian television.

Bindi's nomination for "Most Popular Female Television Presenter" is testament to her exceptional talent and undeniable appeal as a host. Her genuine love for animals combined with her magnetic personality has endeared her to viewers of all ages. From hosting wildlife-focused shows to sharing conservation messages through various media platforms, Bindi has become a role model for aspiring presenters while simultaneously capturing the hearts of millions around the world.

Beyond her impressive presentation skills, Bindi's dedication to wildlife conservation is truly awe-inspiring. Following in her father's footsteps, she has become an influential advocate for the protection and preservation of our planet's incredible biodiversity. Through her television appearances and environmental activism, Bindi strives to raise awareness about the urgent need to safeguard our natural world for future generations.

Bindi's impact extends far beyond the realm of television. Her ability to connect with young viewers resonates deeply, inspiring them to take an active role in protecting and appreciating nature. By encouraging children and adults alike to embrace their passion for wildlife and make positive changes in their own lives, Bindi has become a catalyst for change and a beacon of hope.

As we await the results of the TV Week Logie Awards, it is essential to recognize the significance of Bindi's nomination for "Most Popular Female Television Presenter." This prestigious honor not only acknowledges her exceptional talent but also serves as a reminder of her unwavering commitment to educating, entertaining, and inspiring audiences worldwide.

Bindi's journey from a young girl with a passion for wildlife to a celebrated presenter has been nothing short of remarkable. With her infectious charm, genuine love for animals, and dedication to conservation, she continues to leave an indelible mark on both the television industry and the hearts of people around the world. Whether or not she takes home the coveted Logie Award, Bindi will undoubtedly continue making waves and inspiring future generations through her remarkable achievements.

8

CHAPTER 8

In late 2013, a momentous victory was achieved by Bindi and her family in their tireless efforts to protect the Steve Irwin Wildlife Reserve. This conservation area, dedicated to the memory of the legendary wildlife enthusiast Steve Irwin, had been under threat due to plans for bauxite strip mining. However, after a six-year campaign, Bindi successfully halted these destructive plans, ensuring the preservation of this precious ecosystem.

The Steve Irwin Wildlife Reserve spans over 330,000 acres (133,500 hectares) in Queensland, Australia. Its diverse ecosystems include wetlands, grasslands, and pristine forests that provide vital habitats for an array of unique flora and fauna. It is home to numerous endangered species and serves as a crucial corridor for wildlife movement.

The battle against bauxite strip mining on the Steve Irwin Wildlife Reserve began when plans were announced by mining companies aiming to exploit its rich resources. For Bindi and her family, this posed an existential threat not only to their beloved reserve but also to the legacy of Steve himself.

For six long years, Bindi spearheaded a passionate campaign with unwavering determination. She rallied support from environmental organizations, engaged in public advocacy work, and utilized her platform as a prominent conservationist to raise awareness about the imminent danger facing this precious ecosystem.

Bindi's campaign to protect the Steve Irwin Wildlife Reserve was not a solitary endeavor. Her family, including her mother Terri and brother Robert, stood firmly by her side throughout this arduous journey. The Irwins have long been recognized as environmental champions, carrying on Steve's legacy of wildlife conservation.

Together, they tirelessly fought to highlight the ecological significance of the reserve and the devastating consequences that bauxite strip mining would bring. Their unwavering commitment garnered widespread support from both local communities and global conservationists.

After years of relentless advocacy and public pressure, Bindi finally achieved a momentous victory for wildlife conservation. In 2013, the Queensland State Government made an official announcement stating that the Steve Irwin Wildlife Reserve would be protected from bauxite strip mining.

The news brought overwhelming joy and relief to Bindi, her family, and all those who had lent their voices to this crucial cause. It was a testament to their dedication and unwavering belief in the importance of preserving our natural heritage for future generations.

The successful end to the campaign against bauxite strip mining on the Steve Irwin Wildlife Reserve stands as a shining example of what can be accomplished through passion, perseverance, and collective action. Bindi's unwavering commitment has cemented her own legacy as a formidable force in wildlife conservation.

Beyond protecting a single reserve, Bindi's triumph serves as an inspiration for us all to stand up for what we believe in. It reminds us of our responsibility to safeguard our planet's irreplaceable ecosystems and preserve them for generations yet unborn.

The story of how Bindi ended a six-year campaign to prevent bauxite strip mining on the Steve Irwin Wildlife Reserve is not just a tale of victory; it is a testament to the power of determination and the enduring impact of one family's dedication to conservation. Let us celebrate this triumph and be inspired to protect and cherish the natural wonders that surround us.

On April 18, 2013, something truly remarkable happened at the iconic Gardens by the Bay in Singapore. Discovery Asia had the honor of hosting Bindi and her family as they continued Steve's mission of wildlife conservation. This extraordinary event not only celebrated Bindi's dedication to carrying on her father's legacy but also highlighted the importance of preserving our natural world.

The event hosted by Discovery Asia at Gardens by the Bay served as a tribute to Steve's incredible legacy while showcasing Bindi's unwavering commitment to animal advocacy. Even after his untimely passing, his daughter Bindi has taken up his mantle, dedicating herself to continuing his important mission.

Nestled amidst Singapore's urban landscape, Gardens by the Bay stands as a magnificent testament to nature's resilience. Spanning over 250 acres, this futuristic garden is a harmonious blend of technology and horticulture. Its mesmerizing

Supertrees, lush flower domes, and tranquil lakes provide an enchanting backdrop for any occasion.

Terri, Robert and Bindi Irwin hugging a Tree at Singapore's Garden by the Bay, as part of her conservation efforts (Photo credit to: Discovery Kids)

During this special event, Bindi and her family immersed themselves in the captivating beauty of Gardens by the Bay. Surrounded by serene greenery and breathtaking floral displays, they experienced firsthand how nature can heal and inspire.

Bindi embarked on an Asian tour that took her across

Singapore, Hong Kong, Manila, and Kuala Lumpur. This tour served as a platform for her to raise awareness about the Steve Irwin Wildlife Warriors and the urgent need for wildlife conservation in the region.

In each city, Bindi engaged with local communities, sharing her father's message of environmental stewardship and inspiring individuals to take action. By collaborating with Discovery Asia, Bindi was able to reach a broader audience and ignite a passion for wildlife conservation among people from diverse backgrounds.

As part of the event at Gardens by the Bay, Discovery Asia organized a special ceremony to celebrate Bindi Irwin's extraordinary achievements. A tree was planted in her honor, symbolizing growth, resilience, and the enduring legacy she carries forward.

This act of planting trees not only pays tribute to Bindi but also serves as a call to action for all who witness it. It reminds us that we each have a role to play in creating a sustainable future for generations to come.

The event hosted by Discovery Asia at Gardens by the Bay was more than just an occasion; it was a testament to the power of one family's unwavering commitment to wildlife conservation. Through Bindi's tireless efforts, Steve Irwin's mission lives on, inspiring millions around the world.

As adults passionate about our planet's well-being, let us embrace Bindi's message and take action to protect the precious biodiversity that surrounds us. Together, we can create a world where future generations can marvel at the wonders of nature, just as Steve and Bindi have shown us.

Bindi emerged as a remarkable young woman in her own right. In 2013, she was recognized as one of the 125 Leading Women by the YWCA Queensland. This prestigious accolade not only acknowledges Bindi's achievements but also highlights her profound impact on society and her commitment to conservation. Join us as we delve into Bindi Irwin's journey, her remarkable accomplishments, and why she continues to inspire people around the world.

From a tender age, Bindi developed a deep-rooted passion for wildlife and environmental conservation. Growing up at Australia Zoo, founded by her grandparents, Terri and the late Steve Irwin, Bindi had a unique upbringing that allowed her to foster a strong connection with animals and nature. This early exposure laid the foundation for her unwavering dedication to protecting our planet.

Following in her father's footsteps, Bindi became actively

involved in wildlife conservation efforts at a young age. Her advocacy work has taken her across continents, raising awareness about endangered species and their habitats. Through initiatives like "Bindi's Bootcamp" and "Generation Nature," Bindi empowers young people to become wildlife warriors themselves, inspiring them to take action for a sustainable future.

In addition to her conservation work, Bindi found success on television with shows like "Bindi: The Jungle Girl" and "Crikey! It's the Irwins." These platforms provided her with an opportunity to educate audiences about wildlife while showcasing her infectious enthusiasm and undeniable charisma. Through these programs, she captured hearts worldwide and became a role model for aspiring conservationists.

Bindi's impact extends beyond television screens and environmental initiatives. She leverages her influence to champion causes close to her heart and bring attention to pressing issues.

Bindi's ability to connect with young people is unparalleled. Her positive energy, authenticity, and genuine love for animals resonate with children and teenagers globally. Through her various projects, she encourages the next generation to embrace their passions, make a difference, and never underestimate their ability to effect change.

As one of the 125 Leading Women of 2013 recognized by YCWA Queensland, Bindi joined a prestigious group of trailblazing women who have made significant contributions in various fields. This honor not only celebrates Bindi's accomplishments but also serves as an inspiration for women everywhere. By breaking barriers and challenging stereotypes, Bindi reminds us that gender should never hinder one's aspirations or potential for greatness.

Bindi's dedication to wildlife conservation and her unwavering commitment to making a positive impact have solidified her place as an influential figure in the world. Her relentless efforts continue to shape the future of environmental activism.

Through her work on television, Bindi has educated millions about the wonders of nature while entertaining audiences worldwide. She has captured hearts with her infectious passion and unwavering commitment to preserving our planet's biodiversity.

Bindi carries on the legacy of her father who was known for his boundless enthusiasm for wildlife conservation. By continuing his work and amplifying his message, she ensures that his spirit lives on through generations to come.

Bindi's recognition as one of the 125 Leading Women by YCWA Queensland in 2013 is a testament to her extraordinary achievements and dedication to creating a better world. From advocating for wildlife conservation to inspiring young people and empowering women, Bindi's impact extends far beyond her years. She reminds us that age is no barrier to making a difference and encourages us all to embrace our passions, protect the natural world, and leave a lasting legacy of compassion and environmental stewardship. Let Bindi's story serve as an inspiration for us to follow our dreams and work towards a more sustainable future.

In 2013, a heartwarming and unexpected event took place on the popular Australian TV series, Big Brother. Bindi made a brief appearance to surprise one of the housemates, Tim. This special moment left an indelible mark on both the contestants and viewers alike.

During the 2013 season of Big Brother Australia, contestant Tim Dormer developed quite a fondness for Bindi. He frequently mentioned her throughout his time in the house and expressed his admiration for her work as a Wildlife Warrior. Little did he know that his kind words were about to be reciprocated in a remarkable way.

In an emotional twist orchestrated by the show's producers, Bindi Irwin surprised Tim during a live episode. As he sat in the Big Brother house, unaware of what was about to unfold, Bindi appeared on the screen and addressed him directly. With her signature smile, she thanked Tim for his support and commended him for being an incredible Wildlife Warrior himself. The sheer surprise and joy on Tim's face were palpable, as he beamed with delight at this unexpected encounter.

While this moment may have seemed like just another memorable reality TV scene, its significance extends far beyond the realm of entertainment. Bindi's appearance on Big Brother served as a poignant reminder of her father's legacy and the impact he made worldwide. It showcased Bindi's own dedication to conservation and her ability to inspire others through her work.

Moreover, this heartfelt exchange highlighted the power of television in bringing people together and fostering connections. In that fleeting moment on live television, Bindi not only touched Tim's heart but also left an impression on countless viewers watching from their homes. It served as a testament to the enduring influence of Steve Irwin's message of wildlife conservation and the continued efforts carried out by his family.

One of the most significant outcomes of Bindi's surprise appearance is the inspiration it sparked in a new generation of Wildlife Warriors. By seeing someone like Bindi, who has dedicated her life to protecting animals and their habitats, young adults were reminded that they too can make a difference.

Bindi's appearance on Big Brother encouraged viewers to reflect on their own passions and consider how they could contribute positively to society. Her infectious enthusiasm ignited a flame within many hearts, motivating them to take action in protecting our planet and its precious wildlife.

Bindi's surprise appearance on Australian TV series Big Brother in 2013 left an indelible mark on the show's contestants and viewers alike. It showcased her unwavering commitment to wildlife conservation, while also reminding us of the enduring legacy left by her father, Steve Irwin. This heartwarming moment not only entertained audiences but also inspired a new generation to become Wildlife Warriors themselves. Through television, Bindi continues to touch lives and spread her message of love and protection for our natural world.

On August 10, 2013, Katy Perry released her empowering anthem "Roar," a song that resonated with millions of listeners around the world. Little did we know at the time, but this chart-topping hit would not only become an anthem for personal empowerment but also shed light on the incredible work and legacy of Bindi.

"Roar," with its catchy melody and powerful lyrics, quickly became an anthem for individuals seeking strength and self-assurance. The song encourages listeners to find their voice, embrace their inner power, and stand up for themselves in the face of adversity. But what many may not realize is that "Roar" was inspired by Bindi's remarkable life.

Katy Perry singing her Roar song in her music video at the Los Angeles County Arboretum and Botanic Gardens (Photo credit: Grady Hall and Mark Kudsi

Bindi has been a beacon of inspiration since her early years. Growing up in Australia Zoo surrounded by wildlife and passionate about advocating for animals, she embodies resilience, compassion, and fearlessness – values that perfectly align with the spirit of "Roar."

Katy Perry has spoken openly about how she drew inspiration from Bindi's life when creating the music video for "Roar." In fact, she described it as being themed around the Irwins' lifestyle—a tribute to their dedication towards wildlife conservation.

Through her television appearances and public speaking engagements, Bindi has consistently advocated for wildlife conservation while honoring her father's legacy. She has used her platform to raise awareness about the importance of protecting our planet and its inhabitants. Katy Perry recognized this passion and sought to celebrate it in the "Roar" music video, intertwining Bindi's mission with her empowering lyrics.

Beyond the inspiration behind "Roar," Bindi has continued to make a significant impact on environmental conservation. Let's explore some of the remarkable work she has undertaken.

Bindi, along with her mother Terri and brother Robert, founded Wildlife Warriors as a tribute to Steve Irwin's conservation efforts. This organization focuses on wildlife conservation and habitat preservation while also providing care for injured animals.

As a passionate advocate for animal welfare, Bindi uses her influence to inspire others to take action. Through various initiatives such as her television appearances, social media presence, and public speaking engagements, she encourages individuals worldwide to become eco-warriors – making small changes in their daily lives that collectively create a significant impact on our planet.

Since its release in 2013, "Roar" continues to resonate with audiences of all ages. Its uplifting message serves as a reminder that each one of us possesses strength and resilience within ourselves. As we reflect on the song's enduring popularity, we can't help but appreciate how it has not only inspired personal growth but also shed light on important causes like wildlife conservation.

Katy Perry's "Roar" brought Bindi's incredible story into the spotlight, showcasing her dedication to wildlife conservation and inspiring countless individuals around the world. Whether it is through the empowering lyrics of "Roar" or Bindi's tireless efforts towards preserving our natural world, both have left an indelible mark on popular culture and environmental activism. Let us carry forward their message of empowerment and conservation, ensuring a brighter future for generations to come.

Katy Perry's hit song "Roar" not only captivated listeners with its empowering lyrics but also shed light on the inspiring legacy of Bindi. Through her work in wildlife conservation, Bindi continues to make a significant impact, carrying forward the mission of her late father, Steve Irwin. Together, Katy Perry and Bindi have shown us the power of music and activism in creating positive change. Let their stories serve as a reminder to embrace our inner strength and contribute towards a better world for all living beings.

In the vast world of Hollywood romances, there are few love stories as heartwarming and inspiring as that of Bindi and Chandler Powell. While their names may ring a bell for many, not everyone is aware of the charming tale behind their relationship.

It was in late 2013 that fate intervened, bringing Bindi and Chandler together. As teenagers with a shared passion for wildlife and the great outdoors, they crossed paths during one of Bindi's wildlife shows at Australia Zoo. Little did they know that this initial meeting would plant the seeds for a blossoming romance in years to come.

After their first encounter, Bindi and Chandler continued to stay in touch. Despite living thousands of miles apart – with Bindi residing in Australia while Chandler called Florida home – their connection remained strong. Regular video chats and heartfelt messages allowed them to nurture a friendship that would eventually evolve into something more profound.

By 2015, it became clear that what Bindi and Chandler shared was more than just friendship. They officially announced their romantic relationship, capturing the hearts of fans worldwide with their adorable chemistry. Their love story unfolded against a backdrop of breathtaking adventures, from exploring nature's wonders to embarking on exciting escapades together.

Like any couple navigating the trials and tribulations of life in the public eye, Bindi and Chandler faced their fair share of challenges. However, their unwavering support for one another helped them weather each storm with grace and resilience. Despite the distance between them, they proved that love knows no boundaries.

The love story of Bindi and Chandler serves as a reminder that true love can withstand the test of time, distance, and fame. Their journey from friends to soulmates demonstrates the power of connection, shared values, and unwavering support in nurturing a lasting bond. As adults navigating our own paths to love, we can draw inspiration from the heartwarming story of Bindi and Chandler, reminding us that sometimes, amidst life's chaos, our greatest adventures are found in the arms of the one we love.

In the realm of wildlife conservation, there are individuals who shine brightly, inspiring others and leading the charge to protect our precious ecosystems. One such remarkable individual is Bindi, a passionate advocate for wildlife. Bindi received the prestigious Conservation of the Year award from the Australian Geographic Society, recognizing her exceptional efforts in raising awareness and taking action to preserve our natural world.

From an early age, Bindi stepped into her father's shoes as a passionate advocate for wildlife preservation. Through television appearances and public speaking engagements, she utilized her platform to educate people about environmental issues and inspire them to take action.

The Conservation of the Year award presented by the Australian Geographic Society is a testament to Bindi Irwin's impactful contributions to conservation efforts worldwide. This prestigious accolade acknowledges individuals who have made significant strides in raising awareness and implementing practical solutions to protect our environment. Bindi's commitment to wildlife conservation has been both remarkable and relentless, making her an ideal recipient of this honor.

One of the key reasons Bindi received this award is her exceptional ability to communicate ideas and inspire action. Through various media platforms, including her own television series and social media presence, she has effectively reached millions of people, spreading awareness about endangered species, habitat destruction, and the urgent need for conservation efforts.

Bindi's impact extends far beyond her ability to educate. She is a beacon of hope for young people around the world who are passionate about wildlife conservation. By showcasing her own dedication and involvement in initiatives like Australia Zoo's Wildlife Warriors program, Bindi empowers the next generation to become environmental stewards themselves.

Bindi's Conservation of the Year award from the Australian Geographic Society is a testament to her enduring commitment to preserving our natural world. Her tireless efforts in advocating for wildlife conservation have inspired countless individuals across generations. As she continues on her journey, we can all look to Bindi as a shining example of how one person can truly make a difference.

Let us be reminded of the power each individual holds in protecting our planet's invaluable biodiversity. Bindi's passion, knowledge, and unwavering dedication serve as an inspiration for us all to take action towards preserving our natural world. Together with remarkable individuals like Bindi Irwin leading the charge, we can create a brighter future for generations to come—a future where wildlife thrives and nature is cherished.

9

CHAPTER 9

As time went by Bindi was appointed as a SeaWorld Ambassador March 7, 2014. This decision has sparked both curiosity and controversy among the public. While some applaud Bindi's involvement with SeaWorld, others question her association with an organization that has faced significant backlash in recent years.

The appointment of Bindi as a SeaWorld Ambassador can be seen as a strategic move by the theme park to deflect from the negative attention it received following the release of the documentary "Blackfish." The film shed light on alleged mistreatment of orcas in captivity, leading to widespread criticism and a decline in public support for SeaWorld.

SeaWorld Kids – the kid-focused entertainment program of SeaWorld – is launching a new initiative to inspire their efforts and change the way kids look at, and act on, conservation. Globally recognized animal conservationist Bindi Irwin is the new youth ambassador for SeaWorld Kids' new Generation Nature(TM) (GenN), a multimedia engagement platform where kids can participate in environmentally responsible activities, share their actions and become educated and empowered to serve as game changers for animals and nature. (PRNewsFoto/SeaWorld Parks & Entertainment) (PRNewsFoto/SEAWORLD PARKS _ ENTERTAINMENT)

By aligning themselves with Bindi Irwin, SeaWorld aims to shift focus away from past controversies and towards their conservation efforts. Bindi's well-established reputation as a passionate advocate for wildlife preservation resonates with many people. Her involvement with SeaWorld may provide an opportunity for the park to showcase its commitment to animal welfare and rehabilitation programs.

The news was unveiled during a captivating appearance on Good Morning America, where Bindi, along with her mother Terri and brother Robert, made a striking impression in their vibrant khaki outfits adorned with penguin accessories. With Bindi claiming while on the show, *"I'm so excited to be carrying on in Dad's footsteps and making sure that everything he worked so hard for continues for the generations to come"*, *"That's why I'm thrilled to be empowering kids."*

This unexpected partnership between The Irwins and SeaWorld has generated significant attention due to the polarizing nature of the theme park chain. Known as Sea Of Surprises™, these American parks have faced criticism in the past for their treatment of marine animals. However, with Bindi's involvement as an ambassador, it seems that there may be new developments on the horizon.

Bindi's dedication to wildlife conservation is well-known and highly regarded worldwide. Her passion for protecting animals and their habitats aligns closely with her father's legacy. By accepting this role as an ambassador for SeaWorld, Bindi likely sees an opportunity to influence positive change within the organization.

While there are those who question Bindi's decision to associate herself with SeaWorld, it is important to consider that she may have her own reasons for accepting this role. As an influential figure in environmental activism, Bindi likely believes that she can make a positive impact within the organization by advocating for better animal care practices and promoting education about marine life.

While many see Bindi's appointment as a positive move towards conservation and education, there are those who question the decision due to concerns about animal exploitation. In particular, PETA Senior Vice President Lisa Lange has voiced her criticism, stating that "the Irwin family has been exploiting animals for years, so it comes as no surprise that Bindi has agreed to become SeaWorld's latest shill." She also claimed that, *"But plastering her face on SeaWorld's website won't cover up the fact that orcas, dolphins, and other animals are suffering in SeaWorld's tiny tanks after being ripped from their families"*, *"Bindi's talk-show appearances are just a flimsy last-ditch effort by an abusive park hoping to make a buck."*

Lange's statement suggests that the Irwin family has a history of exploiting animals, making Bindi's association with SeaWorld unsurprising to her. However, it is important to consider multiple perspectives on this matter. Bindi responded to Lange's backlash by telling her Haters to, *"layoff"*

While some may question this decision given SeaWorld's history, it is important to consider that partnerships like these can often serve as catalysts for transformation. By joining forces with influential figures such as Bindi Irwin, SeaWorld may be signaling its commitment to improving animal welfare standards and promoting conservation efforts within its parks.

Bindi, as an individual, has dedicated her life to wildlife conservation and education. Her passion for animals and their well-being is evident in her work and advocacy efforts. It is possible that she sees this opportunity as a way to further raise awareness about marine life conservation.

SeaWorld itself has undergone significant changes in recent years, shifting its focus towards animal welfare and conservation initiatives. They have made efforts to improve their practices and provide better living conditions for the animals under their care.

While there may be valid concerns regarding the ethics of keeping marine animals in captivity, it is essential not to dismiss Bindi's intentions outright or label her as a mere *"shill."* It is plausible that she believes she can make a positive impact by working closely with SeaWorld.

Ultimately, it is up to individuals to form their own opinions on this matter based on available information and personal values. The dialogue surrounding Bindi's partnership with SeaWorld should encourage constructive discussions about animal welfare and conservation rather than resorting to sweeping judgments.

It is worth noting that individuals will always have differing opinions on matters such as these. However, it is crucial not to dismiss or label those who hold opposing views as mere "haters." Constructive dialogue allows us to explore different perspectives and work towards finding common ground.

Bindi's appointment as a SeaWorld Ambassador served various purposes – from deflecting past controversies surrounding the theme park to leveraging her influence in promoting conservation efforts. While opinions may differ on this matter, it is essential to approach discussions with respect and open-mindedness.

Climate change, a pressing issue that affects us all, has found a fresh voice in the form of 15-year-old Bindi. She took center stage on October 1, 2014 in an ominous new documentary titled "Surviving Earth." This independent film, directed by Peter Charles Downey, which aimed to raise awareness about climate change and overpopulation, striving to prevent mass suicide. With its confronting soundtrack, powerful imagery, and thought-provoking scare tactics, the documentary has captured attention and generated discussion within the film industry.

"Surviving Earth" presents a grave message: humanity is on

the brink of self-destruction. As Downey states in the trailer, the film's primary objective is to prevent the mass suicide of our species by addressing two interconnected issues—climate change and overpopulation. By sounding alarm bells and awakening public consciousness, this documentary hopes to inspire action and save our planet from impending disaster.

At just 15 years old, Bindi emerges as one of the influential voices in "Surviving Earth." In this climate change film, she represents the younger generation who must confront and combat these global challenges. Alongside other notable figures such as Professor Tim Flannery, Bindi brings her youthful perspective to shed light on the urgency of taking action. She expresses her determination and belief that her generation holds the power to make a difference.

Reflecting on her own journey towards understanding climate change's gravity, Bindi recounts a poignant moment from her childhood. Watching an old black-and-white film with her mother, she heard an actor utter the phrase "children should be seen and not heard." Confused by its meaning due to societal changes since then, Bindi sought her mother's explanation. This anecdote serves as a reminder that the younger generation cannot remain silent in the face of global challenges—they must raise their voices and take action.

The tone of "Surviving Earth" has raised eyebrows within the film industry. The documentary employs confronting imagery, a haunting soundtrack, and scare tactics to make an impact on its viewers. While some may find this approach unsettling, it effectively communicates the urgency and seriousness of the climate change crisis. By presenting humanity's self-destruction as a potential outcome, the film strives to shake people out of complacency and inspire them to take immediate action.

Bindi's involvement in "Surviving Earth" has garnered immense pride from her mother, Terri. Taking to social media, Terri expressed her admiration for Bindi's latest project. As a family dedicated to environmental conservation and wildlife preservation, the Irwins have long been advocates for protecting our planet. Terri's support highlights the importance of empowering young voices like Bindi's to drive change and create a sustainable future.

As "Surviving Earth" prepares to captivate audiences with its thought-provoking narrative and compelling visuals, it serves as a timely reminder that climate change is not just an abstract concept—it is a looming threat that demands our immediate attention. Through Bindi Irwin's involvement and passionate voice, this documentary urges us all to stand up and take action before it is too late.

Let us join hands with Bindi and countless others striving for positive change—our collective efforts can shape a brighter future for generations to come.

Bindi would later make her mark on the dance floor when she joined the cast of Dancing With The Stars on Season 21 September 14, 2015 when she appeared as a contestant on ABC's reality competition series.

Her infectious enthusiasm and undeniable talent quickly captivated audiences. Paired with the skilled dancer Derek Hough, Bindi showcased her remarkable abilities on the dance floor week after week, proving that she was much more than just a wildlife conservationist. However, what truly sets Bindi's journey apart is her groundbreaking achievement as the first dancer born with Down Syndrome to win the Mirrorball Trophy. Bindi's triumph has inspired millions around the world and shattered stereotypes about Down Syndrome.

The announcement of Bindi joining Dancing With The Stars not only showcases her remarkable talent but also reflects her dedication to embracing life's adventures fearlessly. The anticipation built as fans eagerly await the full list of stars set to grace the dance floor alongside Bindi. The official announcement was scheduled for September 2nd on Good Morning America.

Bindi joined an extraordinary roster of returning

professional dancers, including the likes of Derek Hough, Karina Smirnoff, and Val Chmerkovskiy. The eclectic mix of celebrities promised an exciting season filled with unexpected surprises, fierce competition, and unforgettable performances. As she aptly puts it, "Life is about daring to dream." And what better way to embrace that philosophy than by stepping into an entirely new arena filled with rhythm, grace, and endless possibilities?

Bindi's commitment to wildlife conservation has made her a global role model inspiring people of all ages. However, this new chapter in her life allows her to showcase another side – her passion for dance. While she may be known for her fearless work with animals, Bindi embraced a different kind of wild energy on the dance floor.

Bindi's participation in Dancing With The Stars promised not only captivating performances but also a journey that touched our hearts. Her dedication, resilience, and love for life serves as an inspiration for everyone that watched her dance if you haven;t already watched her perform.

As we embark on this thrilling season of Dancing With The Stars, get ready to witness Bindi's transformation from conservationist extraordinaire to dance sensation. Her infectious energy and determination captivated audiences week after week.

Week 1: *Jive to "Crocodile Rock"*

The night was filled with electrifying performances, surprises, and plenty of drama. At the end of the two-hour premiere, two contestants emerged as frontrunners, captivating both the judges and the audience. Conservationist Bindi Irwin and singer Nick Carter wowed everyone with their exceptional talent, tying for the top spot on the leaderboard with an impressive score of 24 out of 30 points each.

Bindi Irwin and her dance partner Derek Hough on ABC Dancing With The Stars dancing to Crocodile Rock (Photo credit: ABC Dancing With The Stars)

In her debut performance on Dancing With The Stars, Bindi took on the lively Jive. Set to the iconic tune "Crocodile Rock" by Elton John, her energy was infectious from the moment she stepped onto the dance floor. Bindi and Derek's chemistry was palpable as they flawlessly executed intricate footwork and energetic jumps. Their performance earned them a score of 8-8-8, totaling 24 points.

Week 2: *Tango to "You Shook Me All Night Long" and Waltz to "Only a Man"*

Bindi continued to impress in week two with not one but two stunning performances. First up was an intense Tango choreographed to AC/DC's "You Shook Me All Night Long." She embraced the passionate nature of this dance style and delivered a mesmerizing routine that earned her high praise from the judges. Scoring 9-8-8, she achieved a total of 25 points.

The second performance of the night showcased Bindi's versatility as she gracefully transitioned into a Waltz set to Jonny Lang's soulful ballad "Only a Man." With elegance and poise, she glided across the dance floor alongside Derek, leaving viewers enchanted by their seamless connection. Despite facing some technical challenges during this routine, Bindi still managed to impress the judges, securing a score of 7-8-8 and a total of 23 points.

Week 3: *Quickstep to "Movin' on Up" with Guest Judge Alfonso Ribeiro*

Week three brought another exciting challenge for Bindi as she tackled the Quickstep, known for its quick tempo and intricate footwork. Dancing to the upbeat tune "Movin' on Up" by Ja'net Dubois, she dazzled both the audience and guest judge Alfonso Ribeiro with her precision and infectious energy. Bindi's performance earned her an impressive score of 8-8-8-8, totaling 32 points.

Week 4: *Contemporary to "Every Breath You Take"*

In week four, Bindi showcased her emotional depth and artistry through a Contemporary routine set to a cover of The Police's "Every Breath You Take" sung by Aaron Krause feat. Lisa Anne. Bindi left viewers in awe with her heartfelt and emotional performance on Dancing with the Stars.

Bindi Irwin and Derek Hough dancing to The Police's "Every Breath You Take" on ABC Dancing With The Stars (Photo Credit ABC Dancing With The Stars)

In an episode dedicated to the "Most Memorable Year," Bindi chose to honor her father's legacy through a captivating contemporary dance routine alongside her partner Derek. The powerful performance, set to the song "Every Step You Take," showcased not only Bindi's incredible talent but also her unwavering love for her dad.

Dancing with the Stars' "Most Memorable Year" theme provided Bindi with an opportunity to pay tribute to her father who tragically passed away in 2006. Through their mesmerizing contemporary routine, Bindi and Derek managed to capture the essence of their shared love for wildlife and showcase the impact Steve had on his daughter's life.

As Bindi Irwin took center stage on Dancing with the Stars, dedicating her "Most Memorable Year" dance to her father Steve Irwin, she invited us all into a world where love transcends boundaries of time and space. Through the art of dance, Bindi beautifully expressed her grief, love, and admiration for her dad.

The dance was a testament to the profound bond between father and daughter as well as a celebration of Steve's extraordinary life. Bindi poured her heart into every movement, conveying both joy and sorrow as she gracefully moved across the dance floor. It was evident that this performance held a deep personal meaning for Bindi, resonating not only with her but also with millions of viewers around the world.

Their choreography beautifully captured moments of tenderness as well as bursts of energy symbolizing Steve's vibrant spirit. Bindi's grace and poise were evident in each step, showcasing her growth as a dancer and her ability to connect with the audience on an emotional level. The performance was a poignant reminder that even in the face of loss, love can endure and inspire.

This extraordinary performance touched the hearts of millions, reminding us that the love we hold for our loved ones never truly fades away. Bindi's dedication to her father and her unwavering spirit serve as a testament to the enduring power of love—a force capable of illuminating even the darkest moments in life.

This breathtaking performance combined powerful movements with raw vulnerability, leaving both the judges and viewers moved by its beauty. Bindi's talent shone brightly as she received a well-deserved score of 9-9-10, totaling 28 points.

Week 5: *A Dazzling Cha Cha*

Week five marked an exciting switch-up for Bindi as she took to the dance floor with Valentin Chmerkovskiy. Their electric chemistry and vibrant energy shone through as they danced the Cha Cha to Jess Glynne's upbeat hit "Hold My Hand." The performance earned them an impressive score of 37, with all four judges recognizing their talent and showmanship. Notably, guest judge Maks Chmerkovskiy was present to witness Bindi's incredible skills firsthand, adding an extra layer of excitement to the evening.

Bindi Irwin and Valentin Chmerkovskiy dancing the Cha Cha on ABC Dancing With The Stars (Photo credit: ABC Dancing With The Stars)

Week 6: *A Rumba To Remember*

In week six, Bindi returned to her original partner Derek Hough for a truly unforgettable performance. Set to the timeless classic "I've Had The Time Of My Life" from Dirty Dancing by Bill Medley and Jennifer Warnes. Their Rumba left both the audience and judges breathless.

Bindi Irwin and Derek Hough dancing to the Rumba to "I've Had The Time Of My Life" from Dirty Dancing on ABC Dancing With The Stars (Photo credit: ABC Dancing With The Stars)

"Dirty Dancing" star Jennifer Grey, who portrayed Baby in the original film and danced the unforgettable routine with Patrick Swayze, made a special appearance during rehearsals to offer some advice. Grey emphasized the importance of trust in executing such a demanding routine. Her presence added an extra layer of excitement and authenticity to Bindi and Derek's performance.

In this season's "Famous Dances Night," several other couples also achieved perfect scores by flawlessly recreating iconic dance moments from beloved films. Tamar Braxton and Valentin Chmerkovskiy wowed the judges with their jazz routine to Janet Jackson's "Rhythm Nation." Andy Grammer and Allison Holker amazed everyone with their energetic jazz routine to "Good Morning" from the timeless classic "Singin' in the Rain."

To add even more star power to this memorable night, Olivia Newton-John, known for her role in "Grease," joined regular judges Julianne Hough, Carrie Ann Inaba, and Bruno Tonioli at the judges' table. The celebrities had quite a task impressing this panel of distinguished guests while paying homage to some of cinema's most cherished dance moments.

Bindi captivated audiences throughout season 21 with her heartfelt performances. Her ability to connect with both the audience and the dance routines has made her a standout contestant. With each performance, she continued to showcase her talent, grace, and ability to bring stories to life through dance.

Bindi's awe-inspiring rendition of the "Dirty Dancing" routine on "Dancing With the Stars" left us all breathless. Her dedication, skill, and undeniable chemistry with Derek Hough brought this iconic dance back to life in a way that captivated audiences around the world. As we eagerly await what other surprises this season holds, it is clear that Bindi Irwin is a force to be reckoned with on the dance floor. With impeccable technique and emotional storytelling, Bindi and Derek achieved a perfect score of 40.

Week 7: *Thrilling Halloween Spectacle*

Halloween week brought out another side of Bindi as she embraced the spookiness of Argentine Tango alongside Derek.

Their hauntingly beautiful routine captivated the audience, set to the chilling Theme song from "The Lost Boys" film called "Cry Little Sister" by Gerard McMann.

Bindi Irwin as a Vampire on ABC Dancing With The Stars
(Photo credit: ABC Dancing With The Stars)

Every year, Halloween brings forth a thrilling display of costumes, creativity, and captivating performances and in 2015, the world watched in awe as Bindi and Derek took the stage on Dancing With the Stars to deliver an Argentine Tango like no other. On that fateful October 27th night, their dance was more than just a celebration of Halloween; it was a mesmerizing portrayal of darkness, elegance, and impeccable skill.

For Halloween Night on Dancing With the Stars, Bindi and Derek embraced a vampire theme for their Argentine Tango routine. It was not your typical Twilight-inspired performance; instead, it leaned towards something darker and more dramatic—a tribute to classic vampire lore. The stage was set for an enchanting dance that would captivate both fans of the show and lovers of all things Halloween.

Bindi's dedication to her craft shone brightly throughout her time on Dancing With the Stars. Her commitment to excellence was evident in every step she took alongside her talented partner, Derek Hough. As they embarked on their Argentine Tango routine, Bindi unleashed her inner vampire with grace and precision.

It wasn't merely Bindi's ability to channel her evil side that earned her and Hough a perfect score from the judges' panel—it was their seamless execution of intricate choreography combined with an undeniable chemistry that electrified the dance floor. Their movements were both hauntingly beautiful and technically flawless, leaving viewers spellbound.

In their extraordinary performance, Bindi embraced the dark allure of vampiric elegance. Her transformation into a vampire was not just about the costumes or makeup—she embodied the essence of this supernatural creature. With every flick of her wrist and intense gaze, she exuded an air of mystery and seduction that held the audience captive.

The Argentine Tango itself is known for its intensity and passion, making it the perfect choice to showcase Bindi's transformation. Her ability to convey raw emotions through her movements was awe-inspiring. The dance was a testament to her growth as a performer, proving that she could master any style thrown her way.

Bindi Irwin and Derek Hough dancing the Argentine Tango on ABC Dancing With The Stars (Photo credit: ABC Dancing With The Stars)

This performance serves as a reminder of the power that

dance possesses—the ability to transport us to another world, where we can momentarily escape reality and immerse ourselves in a realm of beauty, passion, and darkness. Bindi's Halloween Vampire Dance will forever be treasured as one of those rare moments when artistry and Halloween enchantment seamlessly merged.

The October 27th episode of Dancing With the Stars will forever be etched in our memories as a night filled with Halloween magic. Bindi and Derek's vampire-themed Argentine Tango transcended mere entertainment; it was an artistic masterpiece that left a lasting impression on all who witnessed it.

The judges were left in awe, awarding them a perfect score of 30. Bindi's ability to immerse herself in different dance styles and fully embody the characters she portrayed was truly remarkable.

Team Dance: *Ghostbusters Takeover*
In addition to her individual performances, Bindi also showcased her teamwork and camaraderie during the team dance segment. As part of Team Who You Gonna Call, they danced to the iconic theme song from "Ghostbusters" by Ray Parker Jr. Their collective energy and synchronized moves garnered high praise from the judges, earning them a solid score of 28. Bindi's dedication to supporting her fellow dancers

and contributing to a memorable group performance was evident throughout.

Week 8: *A Graceful Foxtrot*

As the competition heated up, Bindi continued to impress with her versatility and grace. In week eight, The Icons week, she returned with Derek for a captivating Foxtrot set to MIKA's infectious hit "Grace Kelly." Their seamless partnership and elegant movements wowed both the judges and viewers alike. Despite receiving slightly lower scores compared to previous weeks, their performance was nothing short of mesmerizing.

With each passing week on Dancing With The Stars, Bindi Irwin proved herself as an extraordinary dancer capable of delivering show-stopping performances time and time again. Her infectious personality, coupled with her unwavering determination, made her an undeniable fan favorite throughout the season.

As we witnessed Bindi's growth as a dancer and witnessed her unwavering commitment to excellence, it became clear that this journey was about more than just winning a competition; it was about embracing new challenges and inspiring others through the power of dance. Bindi Irwin's unforgettable journey on Dancing With The Stars will forever remain etched in our hearts as a testament to her talent, dedication, and boundless spirit.

Showstoppers Week 9: *The Viennese Waltz and Charleston*

In Week 9 of the competition, it was time for the showstoppers to take center stage. Bindi embraced the challenge with grace and elegance as she performed a captivating Viennese Waltz to the enchanting melody of "Roses and Violets" by Alexander Jean. Her flawless execution earned her a perfect score of 10 – 10 – 10, showcasing her natural ability to embody both artistry and technicality.

But Bindi didn't stop there. In an exciting twist, she joined forces with Alexa PenaVega to perform a thrilling Charleston routine set to the iconic songs "All That Jazz" & "Hot Honey Rag" from the musical Chicago. Their high-energy performance left audiences in awe, earning them another perfect score of 10 – 10 – 10.

10

CHAPTER 10

———

In November 2015, amidst the intense competition of ABC's Dancing with the Stars Season 21, Bindi took a momentous break. But it wasn't just any ordinary break – it was to accept a well-deserved award for her unwavering dedication to advocating for the protection and preservation of wildlife and their habitats.

Through her organization, Wildlife Warriors, Bindi has become a shining beacon of hope for our planet's precious creatures. Her relentless efforts and passion have made a significant impact in raising awareness about the importance of safeguarding wildlife.

Bindi's commitment to this noble cause is truly awe-inspiring. Despite her busy schedule as a contestant on one of television's most popular shows, she prioritized taking time off to accept this prestigious recognition. This showcases her deep-rooted love for animals and her unwavering determination to make a difference.

Bindi is not just an incredible dancer, but also an extraordinary advocate for wildlife protection. Her work with Wildlife Warriors serves as an inspiration to us all, reminding us that we too can play a vital role in preserving our natural world.

In a heartwarming moment on November 14, 2015, Bindi, the passionate wildlife conservationist had every reason to be delighted as she received the prestigious Young Achiever Award for sustainability in Queensland. This remarkable recognition was bestowed upon her for her tireless efforts in advocating for the protection and preservation of wildlife and their habitats through her organization, Wildlife Warriors. Wildlife Warriors is a non-profit charity that helps preserve, protect and care for wildlife and habitats all over the world.

After Bindi won her award she took to Instagram to share her enthusiasm, saying: *"I will continue to dedicate my life to making a difference in our world"*, *"I feel truly honored to have won the Premier's Sustainability Award, back home in Australia"*, *"'My deep appreciation goes to Queensland Premier Annastacia*

Palaszczuk for honoring me with this award", "I have donated the funds from this award to the Australia Zoo Wildlife Hospital. Helping to save precious lives", "We must work together to create positive change, and I will continue to dedicate my life to making a difference in our world."

Bindi's unwavering dedication to inspiring younger generations to actively participate in safeguarding our precious natural world has made her a true role model. Her work not only raises awareness about the urgent need to protect wildlife but also encourages others to take meaningful action.

Receiving this esteemed award is a testament to Bindi's exceptional contributions in promoting sustainability and instilling a sense of responsibility among young individuals. Her passion and commitment serve as an inspiration for all of us to join hands in preserving our planet's biodiversity.

Bindi's well-deserved recognition highlights the importance of nurturing our natural environment and underscores the significant impact that one person can make when driven by love and compassion for wildlife.

After Bindi took a quick break to receive her prestigious Young Achiever Award for sustainability in Queensland. She was right back in the spotlight competing on ABC's Dancing With the Stars.

Trio Night was week 10: *Salsa and Jazz Trio*
Week ten brought about another exciting challenge for Bindi on Trio Night. She took on the sultry rhythms of Salsa alongside Derek Hough to the lively tune of "You are never fully dressed without a smile" by Sia. Their chemistry on stage was electric, earning them a well-deserved score of 9 – 9 – 9.

But it wasn't just solo performances that showcased Bindi's talent during Trio Night. She also teamed up with Mark Ballas for an unforgettable Jazz Trio routine set to the captivating beats of "Resolve" by Nathan Lanier. The trio's flawless synchronization and dynamic choreography earned them yet another perfect score of 10 – 10 – 10.

Dance-Off: *Samba Triumph*
As the competition heated up, Bindi found herself in a thrilling Samba Dance-Off against Nick Carter and his partner Sharna. With the infectious rhythm of "Lean On" by Major Lazer & DJ Snake feat. MØ, Bindi unleashed her vibrant energy on the dance floor. Her electrifying performance captivated both the judges and viewers alike, ultimately leading to her victory as voted by all three judges.

Bindi's journey on Dancing With The Stars was a testament to not only her talent but also her unwavering commitment to each performance. From the elegance of Viennese Waltz to the high-octane Charleston routine, she showcased versatility and artistry in every step. And let's not forget her memorable performances during Trio Night, where she mastered both Salsa and Jazz with finesse.

As we cheered for Bindi week after week, it became clear that her time on Dancing With The Stars was more than just a chance to showcase her dancing skills. It was an opportunity for this young woman to spread her wings, inspire others with her passion, and carve out a name for herself beyond the realm of wildlife conservation.

Bindi Irwin's infectious enthusiasm and undeniable talent left a lasting impression on the stage of Dancing With The Stars. Her journey served as a reminder that true success lies not only in winning trophies but also in embracing new challenges with unwavering dedication and leaving a mark on the hearts of millions.

Week 11: *A Dazzling Quickstep*

As the season reached its thrilling climax, Bindi and Derek showcased their skills in the final week of competition. On Monday night, November 23, 2015, they graced the stage with a captivating Quickstep routine set to the energetic tune of "Dr. Bones" by Cherry Poppin' Daddies.

Bindi's routine was not just a dance; it was a deeply personal tribute to her beloved father. Paired with professional dancer Derek Hough, the duo delivered an exquisite quickstep performance to "Dr Bones". With each step and twirl, it was evident that Bindi danced not only with skill but also with immense love for her father.

Their performance left both judges and viewers in awe as they flawlessly executed intricate footwork and dazzling spins across the dance floor. The judges were quick to reward their efforts with a perfect score of 10-10-10, totaling an impressive 30 points.

Freestyle Magic: *Footprints in the Sand*
Bindi's ability to connect emotionally with her audience became evident during her mesmerizing Freestyle performance on that same memorable night. To the soul-stirring melody of "Footprints in the Sand" by Leona Lewis, she poured her heart into every movement alongside Derek.

Bindi Irwin and Derek Hough dancing to "Footprints in the Sand" on ABC Dancing With The Stars (Photo credit: ABC Dancing With The Stars)

Their freestyle dance that truly stole the show. Leona Lewis' poignant song "Footprints in the Sand," carried a profound emotional weight. In a video introduction to their performance, Derek shared his thoughts: *"It reminds me of where you're from and your dad always being there no matter what."* These words struck a chord with Bindi, who revealed that she drew strength from her father's memory throughout her journey on Dancing with the Stars.

Their routine was a beautiful blend of grace, passion, and storytelling that left not a dry eye in sight. Once again, their exceptional performance earned them another perfect score of 10-10-10.

A Touching Viennese Waltz
On Tuesday night, November 24, 2015, Bindi and Derek took the stage one last time to perform the Viennese Waltz. With

the enchanting melody of "Roses and Violets" by Alexander Jean filling the air, they glided across the dance floor with elegance and poise. The emotional connection between Bindi and her late father was palpable as she gracefully embraced the spirit of the dance. Although no scores were given on this night, their heartfelt performance left a lasting impression on both judges and viewers alike.

Fusion of Passion: *Cha Cha/Argentine Tango*

For their final routine in the competition, Bindi and Derek combined two contrasting styles – Cha Cha and Argentine Tango – into an electrifying fusion performance.

Bindi Irwin and Derek Hough dancing to the Cha Cha and Argentine Tango (Photo credit ABC Dancing With The Stars)

Set to the infectious beats of "All The Way" by Timeflies, their choreography pushed boundaries and showcased their versatility as dancers. The seamless transitions between the two styles demonstrated their impeccable technique and synchronization. The judges rewarded their exceptional execution with yet another perfect score of 10-10-10.

In 2015, Bindi defied all odds by winning the esteemed Mirrorball Trophy on Dancing With The Stars. This momentous victory not only solidified her place in dance history but also shattered barriers for individuals born with Down Syndrome. By showcasing her extraordinary talent and determination, Bindi proved that having Down Syndrome does not define one's capabilities or limit their potential for success.

Bindi Irwin and Derek Hough holding up the Mirror Ball Trophy after their win on ABC Dancing With The Stars (Photo credit: Adam Taylor/ABC via Getty Images)

After her win on Dancing with the Stars, Bindi took to Instagram to share a touching family photo taken before her father's untimely passing. The image captured Steve Irwin alongside his wife Terri, Bindi herself, and her younger brother Bob—holding a baby crocodile in their arms. With a caption that tugged at heartstrings, she wrote: "The last photo ever taken of us as a family... But Dad, I know you walk beside me always and your strength lives within me." This poignant moment encapsulated the love she has for her family and the indomitable bond she shares with her late father.

Bindi's win on Dancing With The Stars is an inspiration to people of all abilities. Her journey has become a beacon of hope for those who were born with Down Syndrome or any other perceived limitations. Seeing a fellow individual overcome challenges and achieve greatness serves as a powerful reminder that dreams are attainable for everyone.

The media often perpetuates misconceptions about individuals with Down Syndrome, painting them as inherently limited or incapable of achieving significant milestones. However, Bindi's triumphant victory challenges these stereotypes head-on. Her success proves that talent knows no boundaries and that abilities should never be judged based on a diagnosis.

Bindi's achievement sends a resounding message to the world: individuals with Down Syndrome are capable of anything they set their minds to. By showcasing her dance prowess and winning the Mirrorball Trophy, Bindi not only proved her own abilities but also opened doors for others with Down Syndrome to pursue their passions fearlessly.

Bindi's journey on Dancing With The Stars instills confidence in those who have Down Syndrome. Her win serves as a reminder that they too can chase their dreams and achieve remarkable feats. Bindi's story encourages individuals with

Down Syndrome to embrace their unique talents and pursue their passions with unwavering belief in themselves.

Bindi's impact extends far beyond the dance floor. Through her participation in Dancing With The Stars, she has brought greater visibility and awareness to Down Syndrome, challenging societal norms and fostering inclusivity. Her presence on such a prominent platform has helped reshape public perceptions of individuals with Down Syndrome, emphasizing their immense value and potential.

Bindi's groundbreaking win continues to inspire countless people around the world. Her journey serves as a testament to the power of perseverance, determination, and self-belief. By breaking barriers on Dancing With The Stars, Bindi has created an enduring legacy that empowers individuals with Down Syndrome to dream big and reach for the stars.

Bindi's journey on Dancing with the Stars was nothing short of extraordinary. From the very beginning, she captured the hearts of both the judges and the audience with her infectious enthusiasm and genuine passion for dance. Week after week, Bindi and Derek delivered mesmerizing performances that consistently earned them high praise and standing ovations.

Their dedication to their craft was unwavering, evident in their attention to detail and commitment to telling captivating stories through dance. Together, they managed to create breathtaking moments that left viewers in awe. Bindi's growth as a dancer throughout the competition is a testament to her determination and hard work, inspiring others to pursue their passions fearlessly.

Bindi's participation in Dancing With The Stars not only showcased her incredible talent but also challenged societal perceptions about Down Syndrome. Her historic win shattered stereotypes and inspired millions worldwide. Bindi serves as an inspiration for people of all abilities, reminding us that true potential knows no boundaries. She continues to be a role model for those born with Down Syndrome, proving that with passion, determination, and unwavering belief in oneself, any dream can be achieved. Bindi's journey on Dancing With The Stars will forever serve as a powerful testament to the indomitable spirit within each individual, regardless of their circumstances.

On December 11, 2015, a momentous occasion took place that left everyone in awe. Bindi, who is known for her incredible journey on Dancing With The Stars Season 21, was honored in a truly remarkable way. She was presented with a key to the city of the Sunshine Coast in Australia by mayor Mark Jamieson at the Australia Zoo. The Key to the City is a symbol of recognition and appreciation for her outstanding achievements.

But that's not all – Bindi's triumph was further celebrated with a commemorative surfboard. This special surf board showcased captivating photos capturing her memorable moments alongside her dance partner Derek on the mesmerizing dance floor of DWTS. It serves as a tangible reminder of her extraordinary talent and undeniable dedication. It is also a great commemoration for the work she and Derek did in their competition on DWTS!

Bindi stated the surfboard she was given was a special gift because her father was a keen surfer with Bindi stating *"He loved surfing and my job was to help him wax the boards"*, *"That is the most beautiful thing, I can't even believe it."*

Bindi also stated about her Mirror Ball Trophy win on Dancing with the stars that she would much rather take on a croc than go through Dancing with the Stars again. With Bindi stating, *"I would take wrestling a croc any day"*, *"(But) first of all, I'm going to have to go show it (the key) to all the animals"*, *"I am so thankful for my incredible dancing journey"*, *"It really does feel like I've just woken up from a crazy beautiful dream, but even though LA was amazing, there's no better feeling than stepping off the plane into the Australian summer and knowing you're back where you belong."*

To win the Mirrorball Trophy on DWTS is an incredible feat

in itself, but to be honored by receiving such prestigious gifts is truly awe-inspiring. Bindi's journey has touched hearts around the world, and this recognition from the Sunshine Coast community is a testament to her exceptional abilities and impact.

Amidst diligent efforts to uncover historical records, a Sunshine Coast Council spokeswoman was unable to find any trace of other recipients that have been awarded a key to the City of the Sunshine Coast. Then it became evident that Bindi stands as an exceptional recipient, with no trace of any other individuals having been honored with this prestigious key. Such an exclusive accolade further emphasizes the significance and rarity of this momentous occasion.

The Sunshine Coast Council woman also commented, *"I've just spoken to the people at Nambour, their archives go back to 1983 and there's nothing there"*, *"We really can't confirm (if anyone else has received a key), someone said Grant Kenny may have received one, but it's all just a rumbling (rumour). "It's clearly very rare and special for Bindi to receive one."*

As well Cr Jamieson claimed that Bindi's achievements were on par with the likes of Jessica Watson, who sailed solo around the world alone from October 18, 2009 and returned on May 15, 2010 to Sydney Australia, just before her 17th birthday.

Cr Jamieson also stated, *"You really have won the hearts of people right across the world during the 21st season of Dancing with the Stars in the USA", "To dance on the world stage and put yourself out there and have courage to do something you don't normally do ... is a wonderful inspiration", "My chest is bursting with pride today."*

Division 1 Councillor Rick Baberowski, whose division includes the Australia Zoo also commented about Bindi receiving the key to the City by stating, *"Bindi's victory was the emergence of a remarkable person", "She's not just won Dancing With The Stars, Bindi won our admiration", "She constantly shows tremendous commitment and determination to be her best, and just as remarkably she brings out the best in those around her", "We should be so pleased we have such an exceptional ambassador for this region, the next generation and the cause of wildlife", "Bindi's performances on Dancing With The Stars have been inspiring and captivating, and by gaining the world's attention, she continues the Irwin family legacy."*

The key to the city and the commemorative surfboard serve as cherished mementos of Bindi's remarkable achievement on Dancing With The Stars. They symbolize not only her personal success but also inspire others to pursue their passions fearlessly and leave an indelible mark on the world stage.

May this honor serve as a beacon of hope and inspiration for all those who follow in Bindi's footsteps, reminding us that even amidst challenges, dedication and compassion can truly make a difference.

Prepare to be amazed by the incredible collaboration that took place on September 11, 2016! Bindi and her boyfriend Chandler Powell, known for her passion for wildlife conservation, joined forces with the legendary Olivia Newton-John for a wellness walk like no other. This extraordinary event was organized to raise funds for Cancer research, specifically the Cure for Breast Cancer initiative.

Bindi Irwin, Chandler Powell and Olivai Newton-John at the Wellness Walk photo credit GIRL.com.au

The setting of this remarkable occasion was none other than the beautiful La Trobe University-Bundoora Campus in Australia. Participants from all walks of life gathered together, their hearts filled with determination and compassion, ready to make a difference. The Wellness Walk aimed not only to raise funds but also to promote awareness about the importance of leading a healthy lifestyle.

Thanks to the unwavering dedication and support from Bindi with her boyfriend Chandler and Olivia Newton-John, along with countless walkers and runners who joined in this noble cause, an astonishing amount of $218,000.00 was raised on that memorable day. This impressive sum went towards Olivia Newton-John Cancer Wellness & Research Centre.

Olivia shared that day how happy she was with the turnout of people commenting, *"The highlight for me was sharing stories with people, when we were walking; I met so many wonderful people and I asked them who they were walking for and I heard stories about Aunties, Grandpas, Mums and it was very heart-warming and heartbreaking, as well"*, *"It really reinforced why I'm here and reinforced why everybody is walking: so we can see an end to cancer and I know we will. I'm very proud of my Centre and everyone working for it."*

Olivai also voiced how happy she was to have the walk held at La Trobe University – Bundoora Campus claiming, *"What a beautiful place to walk, the trees, the birds, I love Australian birds",* "*The nature here, it has been wonderful and to everyone who works at La Trobe who donated their time, I'm very appreciative.*"

It is truly awe-inspiring to witness such influential figures utilizing their platform to bring attention to critical causes like cancer research. Their commitment goes beyond fame and fortune; it extends into making a positive impact on society as a whole.

Olivia Newton-John commented about how the funds raised that day would be used by claiming, '*The funds (raised) today, for the first year, will be split between the Wellness Centre Program which is located on the side of the hospital, a beautiful place, within the hospital grounds where patients and their families can go for treatment and receive wonderful care and nurturing including therapy of art, music, acupuncture, yoga, massage and the list goes on",* "*We have a huge list of therapies and because of you we will be able to add more therapies",* "*The other half of the money is going to the research at the hospital and help to improve and increase research facilities",* "*It's all great, so thank you.*"

Lastly Olivia thanked everyone that day that contributed to the Wellness Walk by commenting, '*I'd like to say thank you, one and all to my family, Fiona, my husband who bought the sun; to all of you who walked and to all of you who raised money thank you and to everybody here and particularly the volunteer's thank you, you did a wonderful job.*"

This collaboration between Bindi Irwin and Olivia Newton-John serves as a shining example of how individuals can come together in pursuit of a common goal – creating a healthier future for all. Let us celebrate their efforts and continue supporting initiatives like the Olivia Newton-John Cancer Wellness & Research Centre that strive towards finding cures and improving lives affected by cancer.

The Olivia Newton-John Cancer Wellness & Research Centre, also known as the ONJ Centre, is a beacon of hope and healing for those affected by cancer. Located at the Austin Hospital in Heidelberg, Melbourne, this world-class facility is dedicated to providing exceptional medical care and treatment to patients.

At the heart of the ONJ Centre's mission is their commitment to advancing cancer research. By combining cutting-edge treatments with innovative research programs, they strive to make significant breakthroughs in the understanding and treatment of cancer.

Led by the inspiration and support of Olivia Newton-John herself, this centre aims to create a nurturing environment where patients can receive comprehensive care that encompasses not only their physical well-being but also their emotional and mental health.

The ONJ Centre's vision is clear: to be a leader in cancer wellness and research on a global scale. Through collaboration with leading experts, state-of-the-art facilities, and a compassionate approach to patient care, they are making strides towards improving outcomes for individuals affected by cancer.

With every step they take towards finding new treatments and enhancing patient well-being, the ONJ Centre brings hope to countless lives impacted by this devastating disease. Their dedication serves as an inspiration for all those fighting against cancer, reminding us that together we can make a difference in the lives of others.

11

CHAPTER 11

Prepare to be amazed once again by the incredible tribute paid to Bindi on International Women's Day! In a truly awe-inspiring move, Bindi was immortalized as a Barbie doll on March 8, 2018, solidifying her status as a role model for young girls everywhere. This special edition Barbie doll is part of the renowned "She hero" range, which celebrates remarkable women who have made a significant impact in various fields.

Dressed in her iconic Australia Zoo uniform – complete with a khaki shirt and shorts – this Bindi Barbie doll captures the essence of her fearless spirit and dedication to wildlife conservation and that's not all! Adorned with a clip-on toy koala on her arm, this doll serves as an adorable reminder of

Bindi's unwavering commitment to protecting and raising awareness about endangered species.

Bindi Irwin as a Barbie Doll photo credit Mattel

Bindi, who is Queensland-based, is one of many high-profile women from across the world who have been turned into Barbies ahead of International Women's Day.

International Women's Day is a powerful global event that serves as a platform to celebrate the remarkable achievements of women throughout history. It is not just a day to honor their accomplishments, but also to highlight the ongoing fight for gender equality.

Originating over 100 years ago, International Women's Day emerged during a time when women were actively advocating for their right to vote and demanding fairer wages. Since then, it has evolved into an annual reminder of the progress made towards gender equality while acknowledging the work that still needs to be done.

This significant day brings attention to various issues faced by women worldwide and encourages individuals and communities to take action towards creating a more inclusive society. It serves as a rallying point for discussions, events, and initiatives aimed at promoting equal rights for both women and men.

International Women's Day continues to inspire generations of women, reminding them of their strength, resilience, and potential. It is an opportunity for everyone to come together in support of gender equality and work towards building a future where all individuals can thrive without limitations based on gender.

International Women's day now takes place every year on March 8 with the day having a different theme each year and it involves arts performances, talks, rallies, conferences and marches.

This collaboration between Barbie and Bindi is truly a testament to the power of female role models and their ability to inspire future generations. It highlights the importance of celebrating women who make extraordinary contributions to society, encouraging young girls to dream big and embrace their own unique strengths.

So let us take a moment to marvel at this remarkable fusion of two influential figures – Bindi and Barbie – uniting for an unforgettable celebration of empowerment on Women's Day. Truly, this incredible tribute reminds us that no dream is too big and no goal is unattainable when we have inspiring figures like Bindi leading the way.

On April 6, 2018 during his royal tour of Australia, King Charles had the pleasure of spending a memorable day with Bindi, Terri, and Robert Irwin on Lady Elliot Island. This picturesque island just off the coast of Queensland and in the heart of the country's famed Great Barrier Reef provided the perfect backdrop for an important meeting focused on marine life and coral resilience.

Before diving into the meeting's agenda, King Charles and the Irwin family took a moment to connect with nature by spending time with a few adorable baby sea turtles. At one point King Charles who is a noted turtle enthusiast had a chance to greet the tiny baby turtles when he even took one into his hand. This heartwarming encounter surely left a lasting impression on all involved.

The meeting itself served as an opportunity to discuss pressing issues surrounding marine life and explore strategies to promote coral resilience in our oceans. With their shared passion for conservation and environmental preservation, this gathering highlighted the importance of collaboration between influential figures like King Charles and dedicated advocates like Bindi, Terri, and Robert Irwin.

After the meeting with King Charles, Bindi posted on Instagram, saying that it was a "privilege" to meet the royal."

Terri, Robert and Bindi Irwin meeting with King Charles
photo credit Mick Tsikas – Pool/Getty Images

Bindi also wrote on her Instagram account about the meeting with King Charles stating, *"Our family feels extremely privileged to have had the opportunity to meet with His Royal Highness The Prince of Wales and other dignitaries today at Lady Elliot Island"*, she also wrote. *"We joined together to discuss important methods to protect the largest living structure on Earth. The Great Barrier Reef"*, *"We must work together to make a difference and protect these sensitive ecosystems for the generations to come #RoyalVisitAustralia."*

Together the Irwins with King Charles, demonstrated their commitment to raising awareness about the fragile ecosystems that surround us. By shining a spotlight on these critical topics during the Royal Tour of Australia, King Charles continues to inspire others to take action in safeguarding our precious marine life and preserving our stunning coral reefs along the coast of Queensland, Australia.

In January 19, 2019 Bindi and her mother began campaigning to overturn a legislation that allowed the harvesting of wild crocodile eggs. Her relentless and passionate efforts as a conservationist, once again took center stage, as she spearheaded a campaign to overturn legislation that permits the harvesting of wild crocodile eggs. With her unwavering dedication to wildlife preservation, Bindi aims to shed light on the detrimental consequences this practice has on both crocodiles and the delicate ecosystem they inhabit.

There has been a growing concern about the impact of harvesting wild crocodile eggs and its potential consequences on both individual species and entire ecosystems. Bindi stands at the forefront of this fight, passionately campaigning for the preservation of these vulnerable creatures.

One of the primary concerns surrounding egg harvesting is its direct impact on crocodile populations. By removing eggs from their natural nests in pristine, wild environments, we risk disrupting the delicate balance that sustains these apex predators. As Bindi rightly points out, allowing such practices can lead to a decline in future generations of these magnificent creatures.

Crocodiles play an essential role in maintaining healthy ecosystems by regulating prey populations and contributing to nutrient cycling. When their numbers dwindle due to egg harvesting, it creates a ripple effect throughout the entire food chain. The reduction in crocodile populations can lead to imbalances in fish and crab populations as well as other species dependent on them.

A concerning aspect of current legislation allows scientific monitoring to shift from independent researchers to crocodile farmers themselves. This transfer of responsibility creates a potential loophole for illegal trade in crocodile eggs, as it becomes harder to regulate and monitor the process effectively.

Bindi's campaign highlights this issue, emphasizing the need for stricter regulations and oversight.

Bindi is not alone in her fight against the harvesting of wild crocodile eggs. Her mother, Terri, has also taken up the cause by starting a petition aimed at bringing about change. By rallying support from concerned individuals worldwide, Terri hopes to amplify their collective voice and draw attention to the urgent need for action.

Terri recognizes the impact that public support can have in influencing policymakers and enacting change. By encouraging people from all walks of life to sign her petition, she aims to demonstrate that there is widespread concern about these practices. The more signatures garnered, the stronger the message becomes.

One crucial aspect highlighted by Terri's petition is the necessity for additional research before making irreversible decisions regarding egg harvesting. By investing in comprehensive studies that evaluate both short-term and long-term impacts on crocodile populations and ecosystems, we can make informed decisions that prioritize conservation efforts.

The combined efforts of Bindi and her mother Terri Irwin shed light on an issue that demands immediate attention—the harvesting of wild crocodile eggs. Through their campaigns and petitions, they strive to protect these magnificent creatures while preserving delicate ecosystems.

As adults who care about our natural heritage, it is incumbent upon us to support these endeavors actively. By raising awareness about the consequences of egg harvesting and advocating for further research, we can ensure a future where wild crocodile populations thrive and our ecosystems remain balanced. Let us stand alongside Bindi and Terri Irwin in their mission to safeguard these apex predators and protect the wonders of our natural world.

The legacy of Steve Irwin 'The Crocodile Hunter' lives on through his family, who have continued to honor his memory by dedicating their lives to wildlife conservation. Bindi, along with her mother Terri and her brother Robert, has been actively involved in carrying forward her father's work that they share with their fans in their show Crikey! It's The Irwins. The first episode aired on October 28, 2018.

This captivating show takes viewers on a thrilling journey through Australia's breathtaking landscapes while showcasing the family's unwavering dedication to wildlife preservation while continuing Steve's Legacy.

It has been over a decade since Steve tragically passed away, but his passion for wildlife and his commitment to conservation live on through his family. Bindi has already made a significant impact in continuing her father's legacy. By starring in Crikey! It's the Irwins alongside Terri and Robert, she not only carries forward Steve's mission but also inspires countless others to join in the effort to protect our planet's precious creatures.

Crikey, It's The Irwins spanned for five seasons:

Season 1 had 14 episodes with the Season premiere airing on October 28, 2018 and the season finale aired on January 27, 2019 on Animal Planet.

Season 2 had 12 episodes with the season premiere airing on October 5, 2019 and the Season finale aired on December 21, 2019 on Animal Planet.

Season 3 had 12 episodes with the Season premiere airing on February 7, 2021 and the season finale aired on April 18, 2012 on Discovery.

Season 4 had 7 episodes and the Season premiere was on January 1, 2021 with the Season finale airing on February 5, 2022 on Animal Planet.

Lastly the Specials had only 5 episodes with the season premiere airing on October 5, 2019 and the Season finale aired on July 11, 2012 on Animal Planet Discovery and the Discovery Channel.

All the episodes were full of captivating storytelling combined with invaluable lessons about wildlife conservation.

When watching the episodes prepare yourself for awe-inspiring unforgettable wildlife encounters with some of Australia's most extraordinary creatures. From slithering reptiles to majestic marsupials, Crikey! It's the Irwins will take us on a wild journey through the diverse landscapes that serve as home to these incredible animals.

We also get a glimpse of Behind-the-scenes adventures into the daily lives of the Irwin family as they navigate their commitments to wildlife conservation and the operation of Australia Zoo. Discover the challenges they face, the triumphs they celebrate, and the unwavering love and dedication that fuels their important work.

While Crikey! It's the Irwins primarily focuses on wildlife conservation, it also offers glimpses into the strong bond shared by Bindi, Terri, and Robert. Witness heartwarming moments that highlight their unbreakable family ties as they work together to honor Steve's legacy.

As passionate educators in their own right, the Irwins are committed to sharing knowledge about wildlife and its preservation with audiences of all ages. Expect fascinating insights into animal behavior, ecological systems, and sustainable practices that can make a difference in our collective efforts toward conservation.

Through their infectious enthusiasm and unwavering dedication to protecting our planet's biodiversity, Bindi, Terri, and Robert Irwin invite you to join them on this remarkable adventure. The legacy of Steve Irwin is alive and thriving in his family's commitment to spreading love for nature and inspiring positive change.

Bindi is actually the perfect person to judge Dancing With The Stars and that is why she appeared as a guest judge during week 7 of Australian Dancing with the Stars season 16 on April 1, 2019.

The show's judge was once a Dancing With The Stars champion! If you're not a die-hard Dancing With The Stars fan, it might have come as a shock to find out that Bindi, everyone's favorite animal conservationist, appeared on the show on Monday night – as a judge!

We're used to seeing Bindi decked out in her casual khakis, snuggling up to adorable Australian animals, but what you might not know is that she's also a sensational dancer who looks incredible in a sequin leotard. In 2015 when she was just 17 years old, Bindi won the American version of Dancing With The Stars alongside her gorgeous dancer partner Derek Hough. So that's what makes her qualified to sit alongside current judges Sharna Burgess, Craig Revel Horwood, and Tristan MacManus and offer her two cents about the celebrities' performances.

"After winning in the USA, I can truly appreciate what a life-changing journey this is," Bindi told TV WEEK. *"I'm so looking forward to sharing my own perspective judging on this special night."*

What made Bindi such a popular contestant on Dancing With The Stars wasn't just her excellent technical dancing skills, but the way she danced with raw emotion. When choosing a dance that captured her "most memorable year," Bindi chose to dance about her father's death. She broke down several times during filming and also burst into tears at the end of her performance, which she dedicated to the late animal lover.

Bindi's emotional journey resonated deeply with viewers around the world. It showcased her vulnerability and strength, as she used dance as a powerful outlet to express her grief and heal. By sharing her personal story, Bindi not only honored her father's legacy but also inspired others who have experienced loss to find solace and hope through the art of dance.

As a former contestant and winner of Dancing With The Stars, Bindi brings a unique perspective to the judging panel. Having experienced the grueling rehearsals, intense pressure, and exhilarating performances firsthand, she understands the mental and physical challenges that the celebrity contestants face each week.

Bindi's journey on the show was not just about technical excellence but also about connecting with the audience on an emotional level. Her ability to convey stories through dance allowed viewers to engage with her performances in a profound way. As a judge, Bindi offered valuable insights into how well the celebrities are connecting with their audience and whether they are able to effectively communicate their stories through movement.

Beyond her personal journey, Bindi demonstrated exceptional growth as a dancer throughout her time on Dancing With The Stars. Week after week, she captivated audiences with her flawless technique, precision footwork, and expressive movements. From contemporary to foxtrot, Bindi showcased versatility in various dance styles while maintaining grace and elegance in every performance.

Bindi's natural talent combined with her dedication and hard work resulted in consistently outstanding performances that earned high praise from both judges and viewers alike. As a judge on Dancing With The Stars she was able to evaluate the technical aspects of each routine with expert eyes honed by years of rigorous training alongside world-class professional dancers.

Bindi's passion for dance is evident in every step she takes. Her love for this art form shines through in her performances as she immerses herself fully into each routine. Her genuine enthusiasm was contagious as it inspired both fellow competitors and viewers at home.

As a judge, Bindi's passion undoubtedly ignited a spark in the celebrities, encouraging them to push their boundaries and explore new creative possibilities. Her infectious energy will serve as a reminder that dancing is not just about executing the steps but also about embracing the joy and freedom that movement can bring.

Bindi's presence on the judging panel added a layer of compassion and understanding that enhanced the overall experience for both the dancers and viewers. Her ability to connect with people from all walks of life established her as an approachable figure who genuinely cares about nurturing talent and celebrating individual growth.

Bindi's role as a judge on Dancing With The Stars is a testament to her remarkable journey as a dancer, her resilience in overcoming adversity, and her genuine passion for this art form. From her emotional performances to her technical prowess, Bindi brought a wealth of experience and expertise to the judging panel. Her unique perspective, combined with her warmth and compassion, made her the perfect person to offer valuable insights while inspiring new generations of dancers to embrace their own stories through movement.

Lastly, Bindi's warm and compassionate nature makes her relatable to the celebrity contestants. Having been in their shoes, she understands the nerves, insecurities, and triumphs that come with participating in Dancing With The Stars. Bindi's empathy allows her to provide constructive feedback while offering words of encouragement and support to help the contestants grow throughout their journey.

Not too long ago Bindi collaborated with Australian brand Tea Tonic to bring you a unique and health-focused tea range. Aptly named 'Bindi Tea Tonic,' this personalized brew aims to not only tantalize your taste buds but also support a cause dear to Bindi's heart – wildlife conservation.

Tea holds a special place in many cultures as a soothing elixir that brings people together and offers respite from the daily grind. For Bindi, it is no different. With her passion for wildlife conservation deeply ingrained in her upbringing, she saw an opportunity to combine her love for tea with her dedication to preserving nature. Thus, 'Bindi Tea Tonic' was born on April 6, 2019- a range that not only rejuvenates your body but also nurtures the world around us.

Bindi Irwin and her Bindi Tea Tonic on April 1, 2019 (Photo credit: Bindi Irwin Instagram @bindisueirwin)

At the heart of Bindi's tea collection lies the captivating blend called 'Wild By Nature.' Crafted with care and purpose, this infusion takes you on a sensory journey through carefully selected ingredients that promote both wellness and indulgence.

The Wild By Nature blend boasts an enchanting medley of flowers, including delicate sea lavender, fragrant rose buds, and vivid butterfly pea blossoms. Each sip immerses you in a tapestry of flavors that dance on your palate while offering floral notes that uplift your spirit.

In addition to the floral symphony, Bindi's tea blend features a refreshing touch of mint. The invigorating coolness of mint leaves provides a burst of freshness, making each sip a revitalizing experience.

Bindi's passion for wildlife conservation shines through in every aspect of her collaboration with Tea Tonic. Not only has she carefully curated a delightful tea blend, but she has also designed a 450ml thermal bottle complete with a loose leaf tea infuser. By purchasing these items from Bindi's range, you not only get to enjoy delicious teas but also contribute to the essential work carried out by Wildlife Warriors.

Sales support Wildlife Warriors, an organization dedicated to preserving and protecting wildlife and their habitats. Fans can purchase the Bindi Tea Tonic Wild By Nature Tea for $15 and the Bindi Tea Tonic Bottle with Infuser for $40.

Established by Bindi's late father Steve Irwin and her mother Terri Irwin, this conservationist organization has been making significant strides in safeguarding biodiversity since its inception in 2002. By savoring Bindi's tea blends and utilizing the accompanying infuser bottle, you become an active participant in the noble cause of wildlife conservation.

Bindi's 'health orientated' tea range not only represents a celebration of beauty but also serves as a testament to our responsibility in sustaining nature for future generations. By indulging in the Wild By Nature blend and supporting Wildlife Warriors through your purchase, you are joining hands with Bindi on her mission to protect our planet's precious flora and fauna. So why wait? Brew yourself a cup of Bindi Tea Tonic and embark on an aromatic journey that nourishes both body and soul while making a positive impact on our environment.

Bindi captured the hearts of millions around the world with her passion for wildlife and unwavering dedication to continue her father's conservation legacy and on Wednesday 24 July, 2019 as she celebrated her 21st birthday, Bindi bestowed upon us another reason to celebrate. In a heartwarming Instagram post, she announced her engagement to her longtime partner and former professional wakeboarder, Chandler Powell. This joyous news left fans beaming with happiness and eager to learn more about the couple's journey together.

Bindi and Chandler's love story is one that has blossomed over the years amidst shared passions and a profound admiration for one another. Their connection goes far beyond their public personas – it is rooted in their mutual love for nature and their commitment to making a positive impact on the world.

The serendipitous meeting between Bindi and Chandler

took place in 2013 when he visited Australia Zoo while on vacation with his family. As fate would have it, he found himself attending Bindi's famous Wildlife Warriors show, where she shared her passion for wildlife conservation. Little did they know that this chance encounter would lay the foundation for an extraordinary relationship.

What followed was a deepening bond built on shared experiences and a genuine appreciation for each other's values. Chandler quickly became an integral part of the Irwin family as he embraced their mission of protecting wildlife and promoting environmental stewardship.

On Bindi's momentous 21st birthday, Chandler seized the opportunity to make a grand gesture of love that will forever be etched in their memories. With breathtaking simplicity, he got down on one knee and asked Bindi to be his partner for life. The couple's joy radiated from their faces as they embraced, sealing their commitment to one another.

A symbol of their love and devotion, the engagement ring adorning Bindi's finger is a testament to the beauty of simplicity. Bindi's engagement ring is made out of an eco-friendly lab grown diamond and recycled rose gold metal. Her ring represents Bindi's environmental activism beliefs and work perfectly. Her engagement ring undoubtedly signifies the eternal bond between two souls who have found solace and happiness in each other's arms.

As Bindi and Chandler embark on this new chapter of their lives together, it is evident that love and purpose will continue to be the guiding forces behind their actions. Their shared dedication to wildlife conservation serves not only as a foundation for their relationship but also as a catalyst for making a positive impact on our planet.

Bindi has carried on her father's legacy with unwavering determination. From an early age, she has educated and inspired millions through her work at Australia Zoo, captivating television appearances, and heartfelt conservation efforts. Chandler has been an ardent supporter of Bindi's mission every step of the way, joining her championing wildlife conservation causes close to their hearts.

In their journey together, Bindi and Chandler exemplify what it means to be true partners – supporting one another's dreams while working towards a shared vision. Their love story showcases the power of finding someone who not only shares your values but also inspires you to become the best version of yourself.

Bindi's engagement to Chandler Powell on her 21st birthday is a celebration that radiates love and hope. Their journey together is an inspiration to us all – a reminder to embrace life's serendipitous moments, cherish the ones we hold dear, and channel our passions into meaningful action. As we eagerly await their future endeavors as husband and wife, let us take a moment to reflect on the power of love in shaping our lives and making the world a better place.

12

CHAPTER 12

____

On November 14, 2019, the world celebrated Bindi and her brother Robert as they were recognized on Time Magazine's 100 Next list. This prestigious honor solidifies Bindi's position as a rising star in her own right, following in the footsteps of her iconic father, Steve Irwin. As we delve into the remarkable achievements and unwavering passion of this extraordinary young woman, we witness the emergence of a new generation committed to preserving our planet and its magnificent creatures.

Bindi and Robert Irwin holding a Python (Photo credit: Axelle/Bauer-Getty Images)

Bindi is more than just a name; she embodies a legacy that has captivated audiences worldwide. She grew up surrounded by nature and an unyielding determination to protect it. From an early age, she displayed an innate connection with animals and developed an unwavering love for all living beings.

Following in her father's footsteps, Bindi has become a leading voice in wildlife conservation. Through her numerous television appearances and public engagements at Australia Zoo – the family-owned zoo founded by her grandparents – she educates millions around the globe about the importance of preserving biodiversity. Her infectious enthusiasm and deep knowledge inspire others to take action against habitat destruction and climate change.

Bindi has made significant strides in advocating for environmental protection. Through various initiatives and organizations such as Australia Zoo Wildlife Warriors Worldwide Ltd., she raises awareness about endangered species and funds critical research projects. By leveraging her platform as a prominent figure both on social media and traditional media outlets, she amplifies her message far beyond what many could achieve.

Being named one of Time Magazine's 100 Next list is a testament to Bindi's impact and influence on the world stage. This esteemed recognition celebrates her unwavering commitment to wildlife conservation, her exceptional achievements at such a young age, and the potential for even greater accomplishments in the future.

With this accolade, Bindi joined an exclusive group of individuals who are shaping our world through their passion, innovation, and dedication. The Time Magazine's 100 Next list serves as a platform to amplify their voices and inspire others to follow in their footsteps. By shining a spotlight on these rising stars, Time Magazine highlights the power of youth in driving positive change.

Bindi's inclusion on this prestigious list not only recognizes her own accomplishments, but also serves as an inspiration for future generations. Young people around the world can look up to Bindi as a role model and see that age is no barrier to making a difference. Her journey reminds us that passion and determination can ignite transformational change.

In addition to Bindi's well-deserved recognition, it is worth noting that her younger brother, Robert, was also featured on Time Magazine's 100 Next list. Like his sister, Robert has inherited his family's love for wildlife conservation and shares it with audiences worldwide. Together, they form a formidable duo working tirelessly to protect and raise awareness about endangered species.

As we celebrate Bindi's inclusion on Time Magazine's 100 Next list, we are reminded of the immense power one person can possess to make an impact. Through her unwavering dedication to wildlife conservation and environmental activism, Bindi has proven that age is no barrier when it comes to creating positive change.

In honoring Bindi alongside other influential individuals from various fields, Time Magazine showcases the incredible potential of this rising generation. The baton has been passed, and Bindi has carried it forward with grace, determination, and an unwavering commitment to preserving our planet for future generations.

On March 25, 2020, in a private ceremony with no guests, Bindi and Chandler Powell tied the knot at the Australia Zoo. The couple's decision to proceed with their wedding just hours before stricter nationwide guidelines took effect was met with both admiration and curiosity.

With the world grappling with the spread of coronavirus, Bindi and Chandler made a bold choice to celebrate their love amidst uncertainty. Confirming the absence of guests via Instagram, Bindi acknowledged that altering their plans was a difficult yet essential decision. As social distancing warnings intensified in Australia, they prioritized safety over a traditional wedding gathering.

"There are no words to describe the amount of love and light in my heart right now," expressed Bindi on Wednesday. Despite having meticulously planned their special day for nearly a year, she emphasized that adapting to unforeseen circumstances was necessary. The absence of guests did not dampen their spirits; instead, it served as a reminder of the broader responsibility to protect public health.

What better place for Bindi and Chandler to exchange vows than Australia Zoo—a location deeply intertwined with her family's legacy? The zoo has long been synonymous with conservation efforts led by her late father, Steve Irwin. By choosing this unique venue for their wedding, Bindi paid tribute to her roots while embarking on a new chapter in her life.

While there were no external guests present at the ceremony due to safety precautions, Bindi's immediate family provided unwavering support. Her mother Terri stood by her side as she prepared for the momentous occasion. Walking down the aisle, Bindi was accompanied by her younger brother Robert, who guided her with the same love and strength their father once embodied.

Bindi and Chandler would later shared their special day on a special episode of the Irwin family television show Crikey! It's The Irwins. Bindi believed that her father was with her in spirit on her wedding day. For Bindi's special day she included her father in a family portrait painted by an Australian-Brazilian artist called the Monkey Brush artist Debb Oliver.

Bindi would later share the professional wedding portrait featuring her dad on her Instagram account with Bindi remarking to The Monkey Brush artist Debb Oliver commenting, *"Thank you to 'The Monkey Brush' for creating such a beautiful piece, it means the world to me."*

Bindi's wedding portrait featuring her father painted by The Monkey Brush artist Debb Oliver, photo credit Instagram @bindisueirwin

To honor Steve's memory, a candle was lit—a poignant gesture that served as a reminder of his enduring presence in their lives with Bindi commenting about the candle and her dad's dog Sui stating, *"We had Dad's picture with his dog Sui blown up on an easel"*, *"So Mom and Robert were standing right next to Dad as we exchanged vows"*, *"We had a candle-lighting ceremony for him, and it really felt like he was there with us"*, *"It was a lovely moment of peace and happiness."*

In these trying times, Bindi and Chandler's decision to proceed with their wedding sends a powerful message: love transcends adversity. Though their plans had to be altered at the last minute, they embraced spontaneity and allowed genuine emotions to guide them. The absence of guests did not diminish the depth of their commitment but instead reinforced the significance of their union.

Bindi's brother Robert took to Instagram to express his pride and delight for the newlyweds. Despite the unexpected changes, he emphasized that love prevailed throughout the day. In a world grappling with uncertainty, Bindi and Chandler's celebration serves as a beacon of hope—a reminder that even during challenging times, love has the power to endure.

As we collectively navigate these unprecedented times, Bindi's concluding words resonate deeply: "To everyone reading this—stay safe, social distance and remember LOVE WINS!" Her heartfelt message encapsulates the essence of their wedding ceremony—a testament to resilience, unity, and unwavering hope.

Bindi and Chandler's marriage signifies more than just a union between two individuals; it symbolizes our collective determination to persevere through difficult moments in history. Their intimate ceremony at Australia Zoo serves as a poignant reminder that love knows no boundaries—even amidst a global crisis.

After Bindi and Chandler married, Bindi would later announce she was pregnant with their baby in August of 2020. Let their love story inspire us all to embrace love and cherish those closest to us as we navigate these uncharted waters together. Love will continue to prevail; it is both our anchor and our guiding light.

The journey of parenthood is one filled with joy, anticipation, and a multitude of emotions. For Bindi and her husband Chandler, this journey has taken on a unique path as they eagerly awaited the arrival of their second child. What sets their story apart is their unwavering embrace of the possibility that their baby may be born with Down Syndrome. In a world where expectations often overshadow acceptance, Bindi's choice to welcome a child who may face additional challenges is both courageous and inspiring.

As time went by the world rejoiced on March 25, 2021, as Bindi and her husband Chandler embraced the life-changing moment of becoming parents. The arrival of their first child has brought immense joy and renewed hope to their lives. Not many know this but Bindi gave birth to a beautiful baby born with Down Syndrome just like her mom. With the cutest chubby cheeks which is common for babies born with Down Syndrome.

Chandler Powell and Bindi Irwin holding their bundle of joy, Grace Warrior (Photo credit: Bindi Irwin Instagram @bindisueirwin)

On the day of the birth of their child Grace, Bindi took to social media to share the heartwarming news with her followers. She expressed her gratitude for having two incredible blessings coincide on a single day – her first wedding anniversary with Chandler and the birth of their beautiful daughter. This serendipitous alignment adds an extra layer of love and joy to an already special occasion.

March 25, 2021.
Celebrating the two loves of my life.
Happy first wedding anniversary to my sweetheart husband
and day of birth to our beautiful daughter.
Grace Warrior Irwin Powell.
Our graceful warrior is the most beautiful light. Grace is
named after my great-grandmother, and relatives in
Chandler's family dating back to the 1700s. Her middle
names, Warrior Irwin, are a tribute to my dad and his legacy
as the most incredible Wildlife Warrior. Her last name is
Powell and she already has such a kind soul just like her
dad. There are no words to describe the infinite amount of
love in our hearts for our sweet baby girl. She chose the
perfect day to be born and we feel tremendously blessed.

Photo credit: Bindi Irwin Instagram @bindisueirwin

Every child's name carries a story, a meaning that resonates deeply with their parents. Bindi and Chandler carefully selected the name Grace Warrior for their little bundle of joy. Each element holds significance and reflects values close to their hearts.

Grace represents elegance, kindness, and divine love. It symbolizes the blessings bestowed upon their lives by nature itself. Grace also embodies the gentle strength that lies within women—a testament to Bindi's own resilience and unwavering spirit. Grace was also named after her great-grandmother and relatives on her father, Chandler's, side dating back to the 1700s.

Warrior encompasses courage, determination, and a commitment to making a positive impact on the world. It pays homage to Steve Irwin's legacy as he fearlessly fought for wildlife conservation. Through this name choice, Bindi honors her father's remarkable contributions while instilling in her daughter a sense of purpose and responsibility towards protecting our planet's precious creatures.

Also her middle name is Warrior Irwin as a tribute to her late grandfather Steve Irwin, The Crocodile Hunter, and his legacy. I think if Steve Irwin was alive he would be beyond proud of Bindi and his family's next generation.

For Bindi, becoming a mother is not only an extraordinary personal journey but also an opportunity to carry on her family's legacy of wildlife conservation and education. Growing up in the spotlight, Bindi has demonstrated unwavering dedication to preserving and protecting our natural world. Now, as a mother, she can pass on these values to the next generation.

Bindi's passion for wildlife and environmental sustainability is sure to influence Grace's upbringing. From an early age, she will be immersed in a world where compassion for animals and the environment is celebrated—a world where every individual can make a difference.

Grace Warrior's arrival brings forth a new chapter in the remarkable story of the Irwin family. Bindi's father captured hearts worldwide with his infectious enthusiasm for wildlife and his efforts to educate and inspire others. Though he left this world too soon, his legacy lives on through Bindi, her brother Robert, their mother Terri, and now Bindi's daughter Grace.

And while many people may have a misconception about the fact that someone with Down Syndrome can have children. In reality a person with Down Syndrome may have challenges in raising a child with Down Syndrome, but a woman who has Down syndrome and is fertile can most definitely give birth to a healthy child not born with Down Syndrome or born with Down Syndrome.

While any woman can give birth to a child with Down Syndrome, those born with an extra copy of chromosome 21 possess unique characteristics that shape their lives in beautiful ways. In Bindi's case she had a 35 to 50% chance her baby would be born with Down Syndrome because she was born with Down Syndrome.

As well, children born with Down Syndrome often face additional complications beyond intellectual disabilities. Heart defects, blood disorders including leukemia, Alopecia Areata (patchy hair loss), cerebral palsy, and immune system problems are just some examples they might encounter along their life's journey. However daunting these challenges may appear at first glance, they can often be overcome with medical interventions and the unwavering support of loved ones.

It is vital to remember that medical advancements have made significant progress in addressing these challenges. Approximately half of all babies born with Down Syndrome are born with repairable heart defects, highlighting the importance of early detection and appropriate medical care.

The first sign that told me Grace had Down syndrome like her mother was when I saw a picture of little Grace's tongue protruding from her mouth. I'm sure the Irwins have already had a tongue reduction surgery on her tongue like they did Bindi's so she can speak easier in the years to come.

Many individuals with Down syndrome require such procedures when their tongues hinder speech clarity due to their size. Although this may change the physical appearance we have come to adore, it will enable Grace to express herself more effectively.

With the birth of Grace Warrior it symbolizes the continuation of this extraordinary lineage—a torch passed on from one generation to another. As Grace grows older, she will undoubtedly be inspired by her family's passion for conservation and carry forward their mission with grace and determination.

In a time when the world needs uplifting stories more than ever before, Bindi's journey into motherhood reminds us that love, joy, and resilience prevail even in challenging times. The birth of Grace Warrior offers hope for a brighter future—one where compassion for all living beings thrives.

There seems to be some kind of big secret about the fact that Bindi was born with Down syndrome. Regardless of this I know Bindi and her daughter have Down syndrome and regardless of the big secret I for one am incredibly happy for Chandler and Bindi's arrival of their little girl Grace. I know Grace is going to be the next generation to continue Steve Irwin's mission and message of conservation.

Grace Warrior Irwin Powell is a blessing regardless if she has Down syndrome. Any child that's born with Down Syndrome is a blessing. Grace was born with Down syndrome and so was her mother born with Down Syndrome, but not one journalist or magazine will talk about this fact. Instead they talk about how cute she sticks her tongue out for the camera.

Regrettably, individuals with Down syndrome often face judgment from others who fail to see their incredible potential. These judgments are fueled by ignorance rather than understanding. Let us rise above such narrow-mindedness and celebrate the unique qualities that make each individual special.

Even Grace's father refuses to speak about the fact his daughter was born with Down Syndrome. Instead Bindi comments how cute it was that her daughter always sticks her tongue out for the camera when her photos are being taken with Bindi commenting, *"Our angel and sunshine every day"*, *"Always poking her tongue out when I get the camera to take her photo"*, *"Grace Warrior, I love you beyond description."*

Grace Warrior Powell sticking her tongue out because she was born with Down Syndrome on October 17, 2021 (Photo credit: Bindi Irwin Instagram @bindisueirwin; JC Olivera/ Wireimage

Grace Warrior Irwin Powell sticks her tongue out constantly

throughout the day and will not stop sticking her tongue out because she was born with Down Syndrome. So she's not sticking her tongue out just for the camera. She's stuck her tongue out because she has Down syndrome and that is a Fact.

Even People Magazine refuses to openly speak about the fact Bindi's daughter was born with Down syndrome. Instead People magazine wants people to know that the reason she sticks her tongue out is because she knows she's getting her photo taken.

I'm the only person that writes about the fact that Bindi's daughter was born with Down syndrome and I'm the only person that writes about the fact that Bindi was born with Down syndrome. I've been writing about the fact Bindi was born with Down Syndrome since 2018 and while I have been writing about this fact I have received extensive amounts of harassment and death threats sent to me through messages on social media.

Unfortunately, there remains a veil of secrecy surrounding the fact Bindi and her daughter were born with Down Syndrome. However, it is crucial to challenge these societal barriers and engage in open conversations about this topic. By doing so, we can dispel misconceptions and foster a more inclusive society.

In a world consumed by celebrity gossip and sensational

headlines, it is disheartening to witness the lack of focus on important stories that truly matter. Such as the extraordinary journey of Grace Warrior Irwin Powell and Bindi, two remarkable girls who were born with Down syndrome.

Despite its significance, this fact seems to be conveniently overlooked by journalists and magazines alike. Instead, they choose to highlight Grace's adorable habit of sticking her tongue out for the camera. Now let's delve into the untold story behind Grace's Down syndrome and shed light on her incredible resilience, as well as the refusal of some media outlets to acknowledge this important aspect of her life.

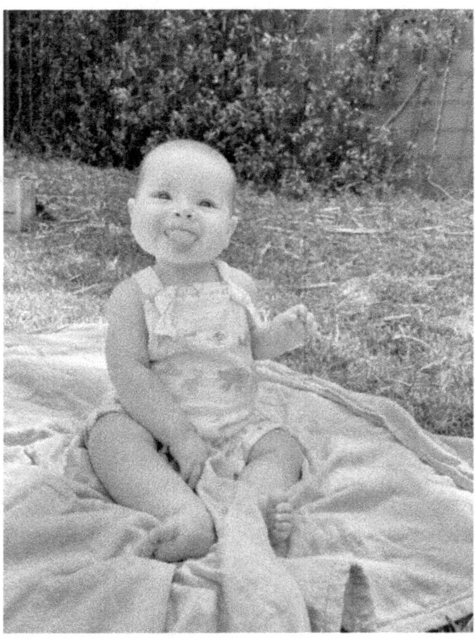

Grace Warrior Powell sticking her tongue out because she was born with Down Syndrome on October 3, 2021 (Photo credit: Bindi Irwin Instagram @bindisueirwin)

Down syndrome is a genetic disorder caused by an individual having an extra copy of chromosome 21. While it affects approximately one in every 700 babies born worldwide, society often struggles to openly discuss and embrace this condition. It is therefore no surprise that even within the public eye, individuals with Down syndrome receive minimal attention or recognition for their unique experiences.

In an era where representation matters more than ever before, it is disheartening to witness the silence surrounding the fact Bindi and Grace were born with Down Syndrome.

By acknowledging Bindi and Grace's condition openly and honestly, not only would it provide comfort to countless families navigating similar journeys, but also foster a sense of inclusivity and acceptance within our society.

Bindi and her daughter, Grace Warrior Irwin Powell were both born with Down syndrome, a genetic condition that challenges societal norms but is embraced wholeheartedly by those who understand the beauty of diversity.

One cannot deny the heartwarming charm behind little Grace's tongue-sticking antics. Her playful nature serves as a delightful reminder that joy can be found in even the simplest moments. However, it is crucial for us to understand that her constant tongue protrusion is not merely for photo opportunities; it is a characteristic feature associated with Down syndrome. By acknowledging this fact, we can move beyond the surface-level cuteness and celebrate the uniqueness of individuals like Grace, who continue to inspire us with their resilience.

Even People magazine, known for its coverage of celebrity news and human-interest stories, has shied away from openly discussing Bindi or Grace's Down syndrome. Instead, they choose to highlight Grace's tongue-sticking habit as a result of knowing her photo is being taken. This selective storytelling perpetuates the erasure of important aspects of Grace's story and downplays the significance of her condition.

As consumers of media content, it is crucial that we demand more inclusive reporting. By urging journalists and magazines to address important aspects such as Down syndrome alongside light-hearted anecdotes, we can contribute to a more compassionate and understanding society.

Raising awareness about Down Syndrome is not a matter of personal opinion but a necessity in fostering acceptance and support for individuals living with this condition. It is essential that we challenge the current narrative surrounding Bindi and Grace's story and encourage open discussions about their journey.

The time has come for society as a whole to acknowledge the realities faced by individuals with Down syndrome. By breaking down barriers, dispelling stereotypes, and embracing differences, we can create a world that celebrates the strength and resilience of individuals like Bindi and Grace.

Grace's journey is not defined solely by her adorable behavior in front of the camera; it is a testament to the triumph of the human spirit. It is imperative that we shift our focus from surface-level observations to deeper understanding and appreciation for individuals with Down Syndrome. Let us stand together in raising awareness, fostering inclusivity, and celebrating the remarkable lives led by those who defy societal expectations. Bindi and Grace's story deserves to be told, acknowledged, and celebrated as an inspiration for all.

Bindi, the passionate conservationist and animal activist who runs the Australia Zoo with her family, launched an exciting new merchandise line, on January 31, 2022, in support of conservation. Showcasing her commitment to wildlife preservation, Bindi took to Instagram to unveil this adorable collection that not only raises awareness but also supports conservation efforts. In this blog post, we will dive into the details of Bindi Irwin's new merch line and explore how her innovative approach is making a positive impact.

As an advocate for wildlife conservation, Bindi is always seeking creative ways to engage people in her mission. Her new merch line is a testament to her dedication and serves as another avenue to spread awareness about the importance of protecting our planet's precious creatures. By combining fashion and philanthropy, Bindi has found an innovative way to make a difference.

The limited edition range features an array of clothing items that are as stylish as they are meaningful. Adorable clothes for infants take center stage in this collection, with each piece adorned with its own unique animal print. From cute onesies featuring koalas to tiny t-shirts showcasing kangaroos, these garments are designed to captivate hearts while promoting conservation causes.

But it's not just about trendy baby clothes; Bindi's merchandise line offers something for everyone. T-shirts, hoodies, and accessories boasting eye-catching designs provide individuals of all ages with an opportunity to support conservation efforts in style. By wearing these items, supporters become ambassadors for wildlife preservation wherever they go.

As a prominent figure on social media platforms, particularly Instagram, Bindi leverages her influence to amplify important messages about conservation. With millions of followers eagerly awaiting updates from their favorite wildlife warrior, Instagram becomes a powerful tool for raising awareness.

In her post, Bindi shared a series of photos featuring herself and her husband, Chandler, proudly showcasing the new merch line. The subsequent images zoomed in on the adorable items, highlighting their intricate animal designs. The response from fans was overwhelmingly positive, with many expressing their adoration for the collection's cuteness factor.

Bindi's decision to launch a merch line that supports conservation efforts demonstrates her commitment to effecting change at every opportunity. By making these items available for purchase worldwide through her website, she is inviting individuals from all corners of the globe to join her cause.

The proceeds generated from sales will undoubtedly contribute to tangible conservation initiatives. From funding wildlife rescue programs to supporting habitat restoration projects, every purchase plays a vital role in protecting our planet's biodiversity and securing a brighter future for countless species.

Bindi's merch line not only serves as an expression of personal style but also as a symbol of support for wildlife conservation. As Bindi wrote in her Instagram post: "I'm so proud of this limited edition range that we created supporting conservation." Let us join her in this proud moment by donning these incredible pieces and spreading the message far and wide.

By wearing these thoughtfully designed garments and accessories, individuals can become advocates for change while looking fabulous. Together, we can make a collective impact and help preserve the natural wonders that surround us.

13

CHAPTER 13

In a heartfelt tribute, Bindi shared a touching photo of herself and Olivia Newton-John hand-in-hand on August 8, 2022 on Instagram. This emotional moment captured the bond between the two remarkable women. Tragically, Olivia lost her battle with breast cancer at the age of 73. Bindi added a caption with the photo of her and Olivia she shared on her Instagram account stating, "One of the kindest and most wonderful souls the world has ever known."

Olivia Newton-John and Bindi Irwin at the Olivia Newton-John Wellness Walk to benefit cancer research (Photo credit Instagram @bindisueirwin)

Bindi's tribute serves as a poignant reminder of the impact that Olivia had on her life and the world. Breast cancer is a devastating disease that affects countless individuals and their loved ones. It is through these moments of remembrance and reflection that we can honor those who have bravely fought this battle.

Bindi's gesture not only showcases her admiration for Olivia but also highlights the importance of raising awareness about breast cancer and supporting ongoing research efforts. Together, we can work towards finding better treatments, improving early detection methods, and ultimately finding a cure.

Let us remember Olivia Newton-John's legacy as an accomplished artist while also acknowledging her strength in facing adversity. May her memory inspire us to continue fighting against breast cancer and supporting those who are affected by it.

Recently Bindi was diagnosed with endometriosis. Afterwards Bindi went through endometriosis surgery around March 9, 2023, which transformed her into a "completely new person." The renowned conservationist has embarked on a journey of struggle and pain, battling this debilitating illness for over a decade. However, her hope now lies in bringing awareness to endometriosis and providing comfort to others who may be going through similar experiences.

It is important to note that endometriosis is a painful condition that affects many women worldwide. Bindi's story serves as an inspiration for those who are enduring the physical and emotional toll of this illness.

In a heartfelt Instagram post, she shared a photo of herself in a hospital bed, opening up about her long battle with the condition. Bindi expressed her initial hesitation in sharing such a personal journey in such a public space but ultimately decided to do so to raise awareness and help others who may be going through similar experiences.

"It came down to the responsibility I feel to share my story for other women who need help," Bindi wrote on her Instagram post. By sharing her own journey, she aims to shed light on the challenges faced by individuals with endometriosis and encourage them to seek help.

It takes great strength to share vulnerable moments like these, especially when one is in the public eye. Bindi's willingness to open up about her struggles shows her compassion and genuine desire to make a difference.

While Bindi's surgery has brought relief and marked a turning point in her life, it is crucial to remember that each person's experience with endometriosis is unique. While Bindi's surgery has brought relief, it may not be the same for everyone. It is always advisable to consult with healthcare professionals because this remains vital for an accurate diagnosis and personalized treatment options.

By raising awareness about endometriosis through her own story, Bindi hopes to create a supportive community where individuals can find solace, understanding, and resources to navigate their own struggles with this chronic condition.

The lack of awareness surrounding endometriosis only exacerbates the challenges faced by those affected. Many people are unaware of the severity and impact this disease can have on a woman's life. It is crucial that we bring attention to endometriosis and promote understanding among both medical professionals and the general public.

Surgical intervention is often necessary to confirm an endometriosis diagnosis. By raising awareness about this condition, we can encourage early detection and timely intervention, reducing the physical and emotional burden experienced by those living with endometriosis.

In a heartfelt message, Bindi disclosed that she had been silently battling endometriosis for a decade, enduring insurmountable fatigue, pain, and nausea. In her candid statement, Bindi expressed gratitude for her recent surgery which has brought her relief from years of suffering.

"Trying to remain a positive person & hide the pain has been a very long road. These last 10yrs have included many tests, doctors visits, scans, etc," she wrote. "A doctor told me it was simply something you deal with as a woman & I gave up entirely, trying to function through the pain."

Bindi's courageous decision to bring awareness to this often misunderstood condition sheds light on the silent struggles that many women face. Bindi stated about her journey with Endometriosis that doctors found 37 lesions, with some of these lesions "deep and difficult to remove," as well as a chocolate cyst. A chocolate cyst is a cyst filled with "dark brown endometrial fluid," according to the National Institutes of Health.

Endometriosis, a chronic and often debilitating disease, affects approximately 10% of women during their reproductive years, according to the Endometriosis Foundation of America. Unfortunately, diagnosing this condition can be a long and frustrating journey for many women. With its diverse range of symptoms and the absence of definitive blood or imaging tests, women often find themselves shuttled from one doctor to another in search of an accurate diagnosis.

In her candid statement, Bindi expressed gratitude for her recent surgery which has brought her relief from years of suffering. By sharing her personal experience with endometriosis and its impact on her life, she not only raises awareness but also provides solace to others who may be going through similar challenges.

"I'm aware of millions of women struggling with a similar story," Bindi wrote. "There's stigma around this awful disease. I'm sharing my story for anyone who reads this & is quietly dealing with pain & no answers. Let this be your validation that your pain is real & you deserve help. Keep searching for answers."

Now, as Bindi embarks on this new chapter of motherhood after welcoming her daughter in 2021, she serves as an inspiration for resilience and strength. Her openness about her journey with endometriosis encourages conversations surrounding women's health issues and empowers individuals to seek support and understanding.

Let us commend Bindi Irwin for her bravery in sharing her journey and hope that her story helps shed light on this often misunderstood condition while offering solace to those enduring its painful effects.

Bindi, a beacon of strength and resilience, has dedicated her life to wildlife conservation and spreading her father's legacy. Sharing her own story about being born with Mosaic Down syndrome would not only empower others but also shatter the stigma surrounding this condition.

Bindi's journey is a deeply personal one, but it is only natural for fans and admirers to be curious about her and Grace's experiences. By openly discussing the fact that both she and her daughter were born with Down Syndrome then this openness can help educate society about this condition but also to educate society on the importance of acceptance and inclusion. Bindi has the power to inspire countless individuals who also have Down Syndrome.

By sharing her story, Bindi can break down barriers and misconceptions surrounding Down Syndrome. Her courage in discussing her personal experiences can serve as a beacon of hope for those facing similar challenges. It is through these open conversations that we can foster understanding, empathy, and acceptance within our society.

Bindi's decision to share her journey not only has the potential to uplift and empower individuals with Down Syndrome but also serves as an opportunity for society at large to learn and grow. Education plays a crucial role in dispelling stereotypes and promoting inclusivity.

In embracing vulnerability and speaking out about her own experiences with Down Syndrome, Bindi has the ability to make a profound impact on countless lives. Her willingness to educate others through sharing her story would be truly commendable, as it would pave the way for a more compassionate and inclusive world.

Every individual, regardless of their abilities or differences, deserves to be seen and celebrated for who they are. It is through embracing these diversities that we foster a society built on compassion, empathy, and understanding.

Society often harbors preconceived notions about those born with Down Syndrome or any other disabilities. Some individuals believe that raising a child with Down Syndrome is an overwhelming responsibility, leading them to consider options such as adoption or even terminating pregnancies. However, it is crucial to challenge these misconceptions and understand that every child, regardless of their abilities, deserves love, care, and the chance to thrive.

By increasing awareness about Down syndrome and other conditions that challenge societal norms, we can dismantle stereotypes and bridge the gap between ignorance and enlightenment. Education plays a vital role in cultivating an inclusive environment where everyone feels valued.

As we conclude this exploration into the lives of Bindi and her daughter Grace, let us remember the power of acceptance, understanding, and celebration. It is time to break free from outdated stigmas surrounding Down syndrome. Together, let us pave the way for a world where authenticity reigns supreme – a world where every individual feels empowered to share their story without fear or judgment.

About the Author

Jane Flowers is a True Crime Author. Occasionally she also writes biographies. She is originally from Greenwood, Mississippi and currently resides in New Orleans, Louisiana.

Her favorite hobby is photography. She has been taking pictures since she was very young and is very enthusiastic about creating and perfecting photographs.

In her spare time, she is a great advocate of transcendental meditation. Her passion is to spread awareness of TM meditation's ability to improve the emotional and physical well-being of your health.